Retellable

HOW YOUR
ESSENTIAL STORIES
UNLOCK POWER AND PURPOSE

JAY GOLDEN

10 9 8 7 6 5 4 3 2 1

Golden, Jay
Retellable: How Your Essential Stories
Unlock Power and Purpose

ISBN 978-0-692-82636-2

1. Storytelling 2. Leadership 3. Entrepreneurship
4. Communications

www.retellable.com

For more information, or for bulk orders,
please contact: info@retellable.com

For Ahrona Joy:

*With eternal gratitude for the care and patience
that you have offered me on this journey.*

For Joel:

*It's amazing what transformation one lunch
at Saul's can spark. Thank you 1000 times
for your partnership, wisdom and mentorship.*

For Izadore and Sofia:

*May your stories always guide you,
and may you also know how to guide them.*

CONTENTS

INTRODUCTION

The Odyssey Begins. Getting to Retellable.
How It Works.

THE ODYSSEY BEGINS

Usually a morning bike ride was just the trick to help me face a difficult day. But one particular morning in the early spring of 2009, as I rode up into the hills, even that wasn't working. I was six months in to my new business, and well into what was then called the *Great Recession*, named for the financial tide that had gone out and not yet returned.

I had given myself a year to make this business happen, but things seemed bleak: business was coming, but too slowly to support my family. Our savings were dwindling, and my confidence was too. *What now*, I asked myself. *What now?*

I pedaled hard up the steep incline of Eunice Street. I felt the warmth of spring and the fatigue that covered me like a heavy cloud—I had been up very late on a production deadline, and up very early with a new baby who seemed to dislike sleep. Trying to push through, I rode harder and rounded left past the redwoods hanging over Codornices Park.

And then, suddenly, something happened.

A scene flashed into my head. I'd love to tell you it was from a story I had heard from some wise man in a smoky café in Istanbul. Or from some ancient text I discovered in a dark cave outside of Cusco, Peru. But it wasn't either of these things. The scene that hit me that morning was from a TV movie. It was the 1999 version of *The Odyssey*, the scene when the lost king Odysseus, struggling to return to his home in Ithaca, rowed with his crew through the dark and cavernous straits between the terrifying sea monsters Scylla and Charybdis.

"Push! Push!" yells Odysseus.

Odysseus's first mate stands up on the ship, waving a torch. Around him, we see nothing but water and high rock walls. Then, CRACK! In a split second, an unseen monster strikes, leaving behind a spurt of blood and bones.

"Row for your lives!"

Another sailor is devoured, then another. The remaining crew rows toward the end of the tunnel, and then light begins to embrace them. The river starts moving more quickly, shooting them out of the cave. But suddenly, the bow of the boat begins to tip. Below lies a thousand-foot drop.

"Hold on!"

Odysseus scrambles up to hold on to a branch as his boat, carrying his entire crew, tumbles down the treacherous falls and crashes into pieces at the bottom, only to be devoured by Charybdis. Odysseus holds on until he can no longer and finally falls, down, down, down, crashing to the water, struggling, and rising again, barely alive. Odysseus is alone; none of his crew has survived.

He grabs a log from his shattered boat and floats on.

The scene ends. And then, a voice. Not quite heard, but felt.

You are not the first to travel this path.

I was still riding, and my face was dripping with sweat. I pulled over and rested atop Grizzly Peak out of breath and disoriented. The movie scene had lasted ten minutes, but it came to me in a ten-second wave of emotion. And, most importantly, something had changed. My body was relaxed; my stress had dropped. My worries had disappeared.

What the heck just happened? I asked myself.

Suddenly, it didn't matter that Odysseus had a boat, and I had a bike. It didn't matter that he was a king on a mission, paddling through the seas, and I was a new dad with a dream, paddling through a crappy economy. What mattered was that a story was like medicine. The story moved me from an awful day to an interesting day. From *woe-is-me* to *whoa!*

Pulled over by the side of the road, looking over the San Francisco Bay and looking down from the precipice of my own life, I realized that, whether it was a poem sung in a dead language by a blind man, a book I had read in high school, or a visual spectacle on a Hollywood screen, there was one thread that ran through them all.

It was the ability to tell a good story.

Since 1995, I had chased the edge of storytelling, through early websites, music videos, viral web movies, web series, and now mobile apps. I had become used to looking off into the horizon of digital technology. In this moment, however, I realized I was clearly missing something. I realized I didn't know how stories actually worked. It seems so simple now, even to look at the words: How a story works. Doesn't everyone learn that in elementary school? Hadn't I been telling stories for years? Aren't stories such an essential part of our lives that we all understand them?

But I realized that I didn't.

I realized I had to start again. That day, I gained a mission: to truly understand how stories work.

So began a seven-year journey to get this book to you.

Along the way, I devised an approach, including a storytelling framework that I believe can help any teller enhance any story. I have coached and trained leaders from Honolulu to Chicago to Marrakech, for companies and nonprofits that are innovating how the world works—including Google, Facebook, LinkedIn, Rainforest Action Network, and the Esalen Insitute.

But this book isn't about my journey—it's about yours.

GETTING TO RETELLABLE

It is no mystery that the social media universe is expanding outward at a rapid pace. Never before have there so been many ways to communicate. Tweets, posts, speeches, blogs, meetings, calls, presentations, negotiations. We're communicating all the time. We're telling stories all the time.

Yet the word *story* is so often misunderstood. In fact, *story* has come to mean so many things that it actually means very little.

While it's exciting to see story as a trending topic, the vagueness of what a story is can distract people from really understanding stories and how they work. "Story" is swapped out for "my background" or "what we do." It's come to mean "our message," "something that happened," or "what we say on social media."

But a story is more dynamic than your "about us" page or a collection of perfectly formed sentences, encased in glass and hung in the lobby for all to see. A story transcends your mission, or what you do, and runs deeper than your brand, or your pitch. And *your story* is not your profile or your list of accomplishments, a depiction of your struggle, or a compilation of your best arguments.

Your story, in fact, is made up of many stories.

And these stories carry your most critical insights and lessons, create profound connection, cultivate alignment across unlike parties, and guide audiences across barriers to actions they have never considered. The ability to tell a good story is one of the most important skills you have as a change-maker, innovator, or business leader.

Because tomorrow, as your audiences and team members sit down for a cup of coffee, they will forget the thousands of data points and news bytes and the nearly hundred thousand words[1] that they drank in the day before.

But they will remember the stories.

They won't have to rustle through their notebooks or search online to recall them, because these stories will be front and center in their memory. As they sip that cup of coffee, they'll ponder the problems you've presented, revel in the resolutions you created, and further the ideas you mapped out. They may retell your stories to friends or coworkers.

And therein lies my litmus test for a good story. It is one simple question:

Is it *retellable?*

The *retellable story* rises above the noise. It depicts an essential change in the world, leveraging suspense, activating the senses, and tapping into the yearning of your audience. It helps you navigate everyday barriers—beliefs, judgments, and data overwhelm—as you find a way into your audience's heart and mind.

And that's what this book is about: The telling.

To help you strengthen your ability to tell stories, we'll explore *what a story is.* We'll talk about *how they work.* But mostly, this is a guidebook to help you *find, shape, and share* your own stories, so they'll survive until tomorrow.

Retellable will help you translate your most critical insights and experiences into something powerful and purposeful, and impact everything you do.

Maybe you're starting a new company or birthing a new idea. Maybe you're facing a tough management moment or changing the perspective of those around you regarding a long-held belief. Maybe you're introducing a customer into a new opportunity, or you would like a certain individual to write your name on a check.

Maybe you're wondering: *what have I really learned? And how do I share this in a clear, compelling manner?*

Not just in your public speaking. Not just in your writing. Not just in your meetings. In every challenge you face, your stories help to guide you.

Yes, I'm talking about *your* stories. Because to harness the power of *Retellable* you must first hold the stories closest to you in your own hands—the ones that deliver your key ideas, your key changes, and your essential lessons.

Maybe your stories are about loss. About triumph. About innovation. Maybe they are about all of these. But one thing is clear: when you can tell them, you inspire others to see what you've seen and what you've learned. You invite them to join in on the world you are creating. Your stories become a vehicle of change, transforming the world from *how things were to how things can be.*

And once you get used to telling your own stories, you'll be better able to find, refine, and retell stories of those around you. You'll deepen your working knowledge of this thing called story, and strengthen the platform on which you stand in order to translate the past and inform the future. Along the way, you'll draw meaning from your life's journeys and communicate them with power and with purpose.

Read this book if you are:

- A CEO, founder, or executive director, bringing a vision to life every day;
- A public speaker, on the lookout for new ways to move

audiences;

- A manager, responsible for leading your team through trials and keeping them inspired;
- A marketer, sales leader, or fundraiser, responsible for transforming ideas and data into tangible connection and tangible returns;
- A communicator, recruiter, or internal storyteller, responsible for finding and shaping stories inside and out to help inspire and guide your organization;
- A person whose official job may not require stories, but who knows that a collection of good stories can only enhance your communications.

Each story you tell informs how the world works. As you bring your deepest wisdom and insights, you place your team members, your business partners, and your media creators on the same page in the same story.

HOW IT WORKS

To help you to find, shape, and share your stories, I won't deliver a mass of theory. Instead, I'll weave together stories, brain science, case studies, and techniques designed to help you develop a deeper understanding of the ancient practice of storytelling as you apply it in a most modern context.

Throughout this book, I will draw on a universal framework I have developed called The Journey Curve, which is designed to help you find and shape any story.

Retellable is not meant to be an intellectual exercise. It's intended to be put into action, to help you build the foundation of a practice. The chapters are designed to be immersive, to hit you from a variety of angles, and to shake up your view of how stories work—all in order to help you work with your stories.

The core of the book is about how you *tell* stories using your own voice. It's not just about how you write them, or how you deliver them, or how you film them, or how you post them—although I hope *Retellable* will help you improve all of these things. Once you can tell them person to person, you can better write them; the opposite is often not the case.

The stories that follow—including the experiences of business leaders in various realms, the folk stories from around the world, and the anecdotes from my own life journeys—are each intended to reveal a lesson that will help inform how you see stories and how well you tell your own. In addition, to keep the creative juices flowing, between each chapter I include a little poetic riff on how stories work.

Developing your stories takes work. While some things can change quickly, much of this work will take time. It doesn't matter if you have a whole team of writers and communicators to help you tell your stories; first and foremost these stories are for you to discover, and for you to tell . . . and they'll evolve with practice. To best make use of this book I invite you to bring yourself—your curiosity, your vulnerability, your passion, and your discipline—to the task at hand. Even if that means five minutes a day of retelling your refined stories to yourself or to others. Otherwise, like a butterfly that has landed on you for one brief second, tapping you into the wonders of the world before flapping away, your progress will be gone.

Here's what you'll find inside:

In Chapter 1, *Making a Memory*, we will wade into the difference between stories and explanations and draw from brain science to further understand what makes a story retellable.

In Chapter 2, *The Thunderbolt Inside*, we'll ask this most simple question: What is a story? We'll look back into history to see why stories matter, and lay down some ways of describing story that will inform our next steps.

In Chapter 3, *The Shapes of Stories*, we take a deeper look at how a story works, and draw from storytelling masters to distill many story frameworks into one universal model: the Journey Curve.

In Chapter 4, *Three Kinds of Stories*, we will discuss the three main genres of stories that leaders tell: Origin, Impact, and Vision. We'll map them on the Journey Curve and explore how they inform your own stories.

In Chapter 5, *Build Your Collection of Stories*, we will set out to find your essential stories, discussing where to look and how to organize your stories and insights based on type and readiness.

In Chapter 6, *The Story-Shaping Process*, we will refine and improve your stories, considering how you anchor in time, draw out details, use suspense, spark curiosity, and leverage change.

In Chapter 7, *Share Them*, we will explore the many ways to use your stories, how to get to the core of all of them, where and how to tell them, and how to troubleshoot when something's not quite right.

As you make your way through this book, you'll become more curious about your storytelling, more creative, and more poised to lead. My hope is that, even in this short journey, you'll feel more connected to your most important lessons and insights, and bring greater power and purpose to your audiences of one or one thousand.

With that, let's take a little ride.

To tell a story is to push off into the river of life, and take us along as you navigate us through the snowy banks, and lead us into the budding life of spring.

Chapter 1

MAKING A MEMORY

The Original Social Media. In the Story.
What We Remember. The Storytelling Drugs.

THE ORIGINAL SOCIAL MEDIA

Imagine a different world: in this world, there are no smartphones, no laptop computers, in fact not even a word for *computer*. No texting. Delete the iPad and the TV, and erase the written word.

In this world, how could you possibly deliver your most essential information to your community? How could you keep those around you from stepping in the snake pit, upsetting a rival tribesman, or setting the house on fire? How could you motivate them for the hunt, or the harvest?

Long before we posted and tweeted our thoughts, stories were told and retold around a fire, in a tent, or on a stage by communicators who offered perspective, shared insights, and passed down essential lessons.

Whether practiced by Australian aboriginals, Sumerians, Hebrews, Greeks, or Native American tribes, storytelling was the original social media. It was made of retellable stories, delivered one to one and one to many, across regions and across time, helping people understand how things came to be and what behaviors would help them thrive.

And while so much has changed, so much has not.

Today, you can communicate with one friend—or with all of your friends—around the world before you get out of bed. You can easily take a picture of a waterfall or a bike ride and just as easily toss it into the global information stream.

And yet, despite technology's ubiquity, we haven't turned solely to data delivery. We still go to the movies, binge watch on Amazon, and are swept away when we hear of a child stuck in a well. Stories are still being told in videos and in posts, at meetings and at meals, one to one and one to many, every minute of every day.

And we sop them up. Not just because, in the information age, we yearn for more authentic connection, but because we love stories—and we can't help it.

We're wired for them.

IN THE STORY

Louis Zamperini was flying as a bombardier in a WWII B-24 over the South Pacific when his plane went down. A bronze medalist in the 5,000-meter race in the 1936 Olympic Games, Louis was known for his enormous endurance on the track, and that endurance may have saved his life. He survived the crash, emerging bloodied and dazed, and made it onto a tiny raft with two of his fellow crew. Their supplies were almost nonexistent: two tiny cans of water, three pieces of chocolate, a rain parka, and three fishing hooks.

The men were withering away in the searing hot sun, in the middle of the ocean. To make matters worse, the sharks began to circle. One man would conjure up his strength to hit them with a paddle as another fished or patched the raft. The men prayed for rain and collected drops in their parka during the rare downpour. To keep themselves distracted, they spent hours on end retelling with great detail the ways their mothers would prepare their favorite meals. Then, they'd slowly eat the imaginary meals. It was all the food they had.

As for me, I wasn't in the South Pacific. I was at my in-laws' home in suburban Chicago, stuck inside during a holiday snowstorm, reading the book *Unbroken* by Laura Hillenbrand. Yet I tensed up as the sharks bumped the raft. My skin seemed to crack in the sun. I became immensely thirsty.

This feeling lasted for days, as I made my way through page after page. Curious, I thought. What made this story come so alive, when others just pass on by?

Véronique Boulenger,[2] a cognitive scientist at the Laboratory of Language Dynamics in France, has offered some insight into this. In a study that explored the power of descriptive words on the brain, participants read phrases like "John grasped the object" and "Pablo kicked the ball." As they read, brain scans showed activity in the motor cortex, the part of the brain that organizes the body's movements. More specifically, the study revealed particular activity in one part of the motor cortex when the action was related to the arm and in another part when the action was related to the leg.

So—Louis was hitting sharks over the head with an oar and scorching in the sun—but it was *my* motor cortex that was activated.

Part of me thought I was there, in the South Pacific, so very hungry, as the sharks circled. I wasn't reading the story.

I was *in the story*.

WHAT WE REMEMBER

Chip Heath, who, along with his brother Dan coauthored the book *Made to Stick*, describes an experiment he ran on his students at Stanford. He asked each student to give a one-minute speech about nonviolent crime. About half of the students made speeches about why nonviolent crime is a serious problem; the other half argued why it's not.

Then Chip showed the students a short Monty Python video—largely to distract their attention—and afterward asked them to write down everything they remembered from the earlier speeches. The students were shocked by how much they had forgotten in only ten minutes since the presentations. But they were more shocked by what they remembered.

> *In the average one-minute speech, the typical student uses 2.5 statistics. Only one student in ten tells a story. Those are the speaking statistics. The "remembering" statistics, on the other hand, are almost a mirror image: When students are asked to recall the speeches, 63% remember the stories. Only 5% remember any individual statistic.*[3]

Facts were delivered twenty-five times more often than stories. And yet it was the stories—not the facts—that were remembered.

So how are stories so memorable, even in an info-flooded world? You'd think they'd just drift away with all the other flotsam and jetsam of daily life. But they don't. Neuroscientist Uri Hasson from Princeton University, who researches how storytelling impacts the brain, has given some insight into why.

In one study,[4] Hasson and his team ran functional MRI scans on the brains of both the teller of a story and the listener. These MRI scans track blood flow, because when one part of a person's brain is active, it needs more oxygen and nutrients—and thus more blood. So following blood flow means following brain activity.

Hasson found that as the stories proceeded, the MRI scans of both teller and listener showed blood flowing to basically the same regions at the same time. In other words, as the stories proceeded, the brains of the storyteller and the story-listener became increasingly synched up. This is a phenomenon Hasson calls "neural coupling." The more the listeners track a story, the deeper the brains align, and the more intimate their connection. No wonder stories are so effective!

Okay, you ask, so how does this relate to my next interview, or team meeting, or blog post, or video? Why does this matter?

Quite simply, when you tell a story—a *retellable* story—the audience experiences what you experience. And, according to Hasson, when brains between teller and audience are synched up, you can practically reach out and place information into the audience's brain.

Once you have the line of connection, you have your audience's attention.

THE STORYTELLING DRUGS

Have you ever heard someone say, "The suspense is killing me!"? Whether said in jest or not, the mere phrase gives us insight into how stories work. Because suspense doesn't actually kill us. It makes us feel more alive.

We're compelled to watch an action flick or turn the pages of a good mystery novel the way we're compelled to reach for one more cupcake. There's a payoff. We hear the creaking steps, watch the doorknob turn, and see the character back into a dark corner as we're drawn deeper into the story. Bit by bit, the details unfold, and we feel the rush of the brain chemical dopamine. Suspense sparks satisfaction.

And, as it turns out, it also sparks learning.

A recent study by neuroscientists at the University of California, Davis,[5] explored the relationship between curiosity and memory retention. Participants were given Trivial Pursuit questions and then had to wait fourteen seconds for the answer.

Waiting . . .

Waiting . . .

During the wait, they were shown a picture of someone they didn't know.

Then came the answer.

Surprisingly, the researchers found heightened memory retention on the trivia topics. But perhaps even more surprisingly, the memory of the random faces they viewed went up significantly . . . and those memories remained twenty-four hours later.

Their conclusion?

Sparking curiosity increases learning. In fact, "Curiosity may put the brain in a state that allows it to learn and retain any kind of information, like a vortex that sucks in what you are motivated to learn, and also everything around it," explains lead author Dr. Matthias Gruber.

Curiosity sparks suspense, which also releases dopamine.

In addition, according to Paul Zak, PhD, author and neuro-economist—studying the field of decision-making—a story also causes enough distress to spark the release of cortisol, commonly known as the stress hormone.

Cortisol says, "Focus on what you're doing!" If you're walking in the forest at night you may trip, so increased attention is valuable. Cortisol is related to fight or flight and will ready the muscles just in case you have to start running away from a wild animal in hot pursuit. But too much cortisol—or a story that gets lost in the weeds—and you're left with an unhappy audience.

So we watch. We listen. Our senses are heightened. And eventually, we get an inkling of the payoff. It looks like boy will get girl, after all. The underdog shows some glimmers of super-strength. A clue is revealed to inform the mystery.

According to Zak, stories also release oxytocin, the wonder chemical that increases empathy, accelerates healing, lowers blood pressure, and eases the experience of pain during childbirth.

Oxytocin also enables us to act with more generosity toward others. In one study, Zak found that when given oxytocin, participants gave 80 percent more donations[6] than those who took a placebo. Makes sense, right? Better story, more empathy. More connection, more donations.

The chemicals all work together in a story, like this:

The wolf arrives at the door of the three pigs' brick house.

"What?" Curiosity. Suspense. Dopamine.

The wolf, finding he can't blow the house down, climbs up on the roof, headed for the chimney.

"Hey!" Attention. Focus. Cortisol.

Sliding down into the chimney, the wolf lands in a pot of boiling water, screams in pain, and leaps up back through the chimney, running down the road, never to be seen again.

"Ahhh." Healing. Payoff. Oxytocin.

When you tell a story that anchors in the senses, leverages suspense, and eases the tension bit by bit around each corner of the story, we can't help but pay attention.

But you must nurture this relationship. If you lose the connection, lose the scene, start piling on masses of data, or skip too quickly through your challenge, your audience can get confused and disconnected.

"If the listener fails to comprehend what the speaker is trying to communicate," Professor Hasson says, "their brain patterns decouple."

Instead of wandering with you down to the river, or hearing the sound of the bear, or anticipating the closing of your biggest deal ever, they're back to thoughts of email, the weekend ahead, and the fact that they're thirsty.

Your stories are alive.
They are not held on the
page, or on the screen.
They live inside of you,
and once you tell them,
they live in those around
you, in their hearts and
in their minds, firing
signs and translating
ideas ancient and brand
spanking new.

Chapter 2

THE THUNDERBOLT INSIDE

Prince Five-Weapons. What is a Story, Anyway?
A Problem. A Journey.

PRINCE FIVE-WEAPONS

A young prince, as a mark of distinction from his teacher, received five weapons along with a new name: Prince Five-Weapons. One day, while walking through the woods, he heard the sound of crunching branches. Following the sound, he came upon an ogre who was known as Sticky-Hair. The ogre had a head as big as a house, eyes as big as a man's head, and arms as thick as massive trees. He had dark blotches all over his belly, and hair that covered him like thick ivy. "What intruder are you? I kill every man I see!" roared Sticky-Hair.

"Not this time, ogre," said the prince, pulling out his bow and a poison-tipped arrow. The arrow flew far and fast, but it got stuck in Sticky-Hair's chest hair.

The prince was not deterred; he reached down and pulled out a club and flung it at the ogre. Perfect aim—but again, his weapon was stuck in the hair. He pulled out his spear and with a running start, sent it right between the ogre's eyes. More hair. Then he ran at the ogre with his sword and leapt up to stab the ogre in the heart. But once again, his sword just got stuck in the hair.

Sticky-Hair laughed. "And now, I will have you for lunch!"

"Oh no you won't!" And the prince jumped up into the air and slammed the ogre with his right fist. But it got stuck in the hair. Then his left fist. Stuck. Then his left foot and his right foot. All stuck. Finally, he started head-butting the ogre, and his head got stuck.

Now the ogre was curious. "Why are you not afraid?" Sticky-Hair asked, looking down at the prince, who was tangled in his chest hair. "Why are you not terrified with the fear of death?"

The prince paused for a moment, thinking. He thought of his great weapons, each of which had failed him when it was most needed. He thought of his many journeys. Until finally, as if beyond his own thoughts, an idea, as clear as day, came to him.

"Why should I be? For in one life, only one death is absolutely certain," he yelled through the hair. "And you see, I have a secret. Inside of my belly there is a powerful thunderbolt. It is my ultimate weapon. And if you eat as much as one finger of my body, you will die instantly!"

Looking down at this brave man hanging on his hair, Sticky-Hair decided that Prince Five-Weapons must be telling the truth, and he let him go.

The prince stayed a while and taught the ogre what he had learned in his journeys. Sticky-Hair became a protector of the forest, and received homage from the villagers. And Prince Five-Weapons continued on his travels, leaving his weapons behind, and in time, became one of the early incarnations of the Buddha.

—Adapted from *The Hero with a Thousand Faces*
by Joseph Campbell

We live in an ever-expanding universe of communications. At our fingertips there are more tools than ever before to help inspire and influence those around us—and we use them, creating messages and media at an unprecedented speed, using unparalleled technologies in infinite forms. We shoot sharpened messages into the air and aim at our targets with powerful arrows of presentations and tweets and well-crafted emails. We hurl the hatchet of our messaging far and wide, unleashing our strategies and speaking before audiences small and large.

Yet so often, like Prince Five-Weapons, these all get stuck in the hair. Our communications can seem tangled, and their meaning can seem muffled.

But we do have something—something alive inside of each and every one of us. We carry a thunderbolt inside our bellies. A thunderbolt! Sound, color, and motion woven into one great force once thought to be held only by the gods. And this thunderbolt is made up of our stories. It connects everything—our insights, our journeys, and our visions. And it is told in a thousand ways, each and every day.

Perhaps one story will be told across a table: a dinner table, a boardroom table, or a negotiating table. Perhaps it will be told across the seas, on a website or across a crowd, in a keynote or a TED Talk. Perhaps the story will start out flat and wander on, without a clear point. Perhaps it will be inundated with data, or simply too forced. Perhaps it will be undercut by telling too much at the beginning, or too little at the end.

And perhaps that will change as you dive more deeply into your story skills.

But before we step further into the power of story, let's first get clear on how we define the word story.

A PROBLEM

Make me care.

So says Andrew Stanton, the director of many great Pixar movies, including *Toy Story*, *Finding Nemo*, and *Wall-E*, in his TED Talk about storytelling.[7] *Make me care.* Make me consider, tomorrow, your challenge. Make your challenge my challenge.

But how?

No amount of information or data alone can make us care. But a well-shaped problem, held in a story, delivered in a journey from one place to another, resulting in some change in how we see the world . . . and suddenly we're sitting up in our seat. Suddenly we're empathizing, and feeling more connected to our own challenges.

This brings us to our first definition:

A story is a problem, approached in an interesting way that makes us care.

But you can't force your audience to care. We're all familiar with team members who continue to yell the problem over and over again and hope to get some different result.

Recently while I was in Waikiki, Hawaii, with an afternoon of rest before a training session, I thought I'd put my feet in the sand. I found a small place on the beach near a two-year-old boy who was digging a hole close to his mother and an older woman who might have been his grandmother. After a while, my concerns floated away, and I began to drift into sleep.

Then I heard a loud voice that pierced my nap. "Oh, yes! Jimmy's doing great!" His mother was talking on her phone about five feet away. "Okay. Jimmy. Now Jimmy, don't eat the sand," she said with a nervous laugh.

Then her voice rose. "Jimmy! Don't eat the sand!" she yelled, running toward the boy. "Sorry, honey, I'm going to have to hang up. Jimmy!"

She grabbed Jimmy, whose mouth was overflowing with sand, and carried him off to the shower. She came back a few moments later. "Now. See this sand? Don't eat it!" She set him down, and two seconds later Jimmy was back at it. She went to the shower again, came back, and finally strapped Jimmy into his stroller, kicking and screaming.

The mom shook her head as she packed the stroller. "Weird," she said to the grandmother. "He wasn't eating any sand until I told him not to."

You can't just hammer your audience with the problem and expect to change them. You can't get stuck in it; you must move through the problem, drawing us in and leaving us relieved, satisfied, and connected.

And once through the problem, you offer us a treasure.

That treasure is your message, the essential spark held inside your story, where your bolt of thunder hits earth. It is this that you pass on to your audience members. That treasure, that perspective, then lives inside of them, as if gained through their own experience.

As Lisa Cron, author of *Wired for Story*, writes: "Stories allow us to simulate intense experiences without actually having to live through them. This was a matter of life and death back in the Stone Age, when if you waited for experience to teach you that the rustling in the bushes was actually a lion looking for lunch, you'd end up the main course."[8]

In other words, we sit up because we have to. We have to decide whether the problem is dangerous or beneficial.

Our tendency toward story is an evolutionary imperative.

A JOURNEY

The problem is something that happens. But the journey is what moves us from one state of being to another. The journey delineates a difference between then and now. It may be a short journey, depicting what happened today. Sometimes it is a greater journey, spanning across years and landing on a turning point in your life, your leadership, or your product. But always, a journey is anchored in key moments, in order to draw in your audience more deeply through the senses and to take them somewhere compelling. There, the world is different. This brings us to our next definition of story:

A story is a journey with a twist, taking us from one place to another place where a change occurs.

The world changes so often—constantly filling us with new information, new relations, and new discoveries—that it can be overwhelming to take everything in.

That's where your stories help.

When a story is rewarding, it creates a journey of change that satisfies our desire to make sense of things, providing a little bit of reassurance that we can navigate the most complicated of challenges.

So we gather these journeys in our stories, as we might fill an emergency medical kit.

Elon Musk, Founder of Tesla Motors, knows a bit about journeys. In his career, he has helped guide many paradigm shifts, including how we exchange money (PayPal), how we explore outer space (SpaceX), and, of course, how we drive (Tesla).

In a recent presentation, Musk told a story[9] that illuminated a great journey. He began with an image of billowing smokestacks. In this, he established the problem: we need a lot of energy to run today's world, and to do it, we create a lot of pollution.

Duh! Everybody knows that, right? But Musk didn't begin by telling us what he was setting out to prove. And we didn't boo him off the stage, because we were curious. We had trust in our storyteller. He wasn't going to tell us about our problems just to fill space. In his opener, Musk simply set up "how the world is now." He then established the solution.

"It's a fairly obvious solution. We have this handy fusion reactor in the sky. You don't have to do anything, it just shows up every day!"

The sun. Solar energy. Sure. But how much solar?

"That blue square right there." Musk used a little social math as he showed one small square on the screen. Just one small square covering the tip of Texas, filled with solar panels. There's nothing really new about the fact that we'll need a lot of solar power, but Musk brings it to a tangible—if still immense—square.

The journey is not over. Because he's getting to the real problem:

"The sun does not shine at night."

This is where the twist in the story comes in. The thunderbolt in his belly. The key, according to Musk, is not in how we capture the power. The solar panels will be built, he said. The twist is in how we *hold* the power.

With a battery. A new kind of battery.

Showing a picture of a set of grimy batteries, he said: "But the issue with existing batteries is that they suck."

Musk then unveiled the sleek new Powerwall batteries, showing how they stack and how many we will need to power the country. But it's not the future; it's the present. To make it real for the audience, he revealed that the entire conference hall was being powered by Powerwall.

The future is here now.

The energy solution is tangible, it's clear, and it's available. The journey has begun in earnest, from smokestacks to a clear destination of renewable power.

Powering a city, state, or country with batteries is no small task.

Yet now we have an aspiration and a tangible sense of change. Musk knew that we needed a journey with not just one problem, but several. Each problem drew the audience deeper into the story. And this story communicated not only the product but also the next chapter of the Tesla story.

Okay. The skeptic in you may be still saying, "But I'm not some billionaire that people will listen to! They don't have time for *my* stories!"

It is indeed important to respect people's time. But in a world where each person takes in nearly seventy-four gigabytes of mobile, TV, radio, ads, and computer data each day,[10] endlessly adding facts and explanations isn't the way to capture their attention.

You may not be presenting in front of a thousand audience members who can't wait to hear about your next creation. But whether you're sitting in an interview and need to illuminate the purpose of your work, mapping out an opportunity for a prospective client, or inspiring a team member to expand beyond her capacity, a well-shaped journey can make all the difference.

A story is a problem, approached in an interesting way, that sends us on a journey. Along the way, in key moments in time, changes happen. The twists and turns draw us in, give form to the journey, and enable us to gain new understanding. And the teller is the guide to that understanding, helping us navigate a new world.

Chapter 3

THE SHAPES OF STORIES

The Story That Wasn't. Getting to a Framework.
The Journey Curve. Using the Pivots.

THE STORY THAT WASN'T

One night a few years ago, I was putting our four-year-old daughter Sofia to bed with a story.

I was tired, and in the coziness of her bottom bunk, I found myself fading into dreamtime as I spoke. I realized I had to put a quick end to the story.

"And then, the little girl felt much better . . . and they all lived happily ever after." And I drifted off into sleep.

"Dad!" I heard, accompanied by a kick in the ribs that jolted me awake.

"What?"

"Dad. That's not a story!"

The fact is, we each recognize a good story when we hear one—and have been able to for a long time.

But we don't always tell them so well. Why is that?

We can drift around, get lost in the problem, or skip too quickly to the solution. We can swamp our audiences with too much detail, or not enough, and can forget where we're going, or we can tell a story that just doesn't match the moment.

There are so many things that go wrong, and dozens of possible approaches. But with a simple, clear frame to guide and inform your path, you can spend more of your valuable energy on finding, developing, and enjoying your retellable stories.

A story framework will help you workshop your stories, map them, remember them, and know at all times where you are and where you need to go. It will also help you avoid a kick in the ribs—either in the form of rolling eyes, a bored audience, or messages that simply don't sink in.

GETTING TO A FRAMEWORK

Ask anyone about the key components of a story, and the first response is often this: something with a beginning, a middle, and an end.

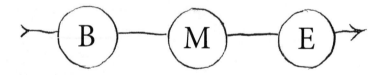

This is true. Stories do have a beginning, a middle, and an end.

We know, however, that a story is not a straight line—otherwise you'd be able to see right to the end! A story is a series of twists and turns that reflect a key life lesson, shaped in a way that draws us in. And at the end, things are better somehow. Something has been learned, something has been healed, and something has been transformed.

But you can't just say it. You have to show it.

Let's briefly explore a few different story frameworks. On You-Tube recently, I discovered a presentation made by American author Kurt Vonnegut back in the eighties. The presentation, about how stories work, was called "The Shapes of Stories." Addressing a topic that writers and teachers have grappled with since time began, Vonnegut's lesson took all of one minute.[11]

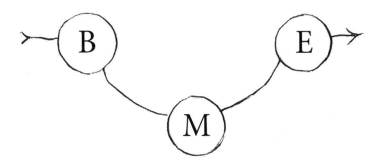

"We call this story *Man in Hole,*" Vonnegut said. "But it needn't be about a man, and it needn't be about a hole."

He took a piece of chalk and drew two lines on the board, one up and down, and one across. He then drew a U-shaped curve, starting fairly high, dropping low into a gulley, and returning once more on the other side.

"Somebody gets into trouble, then gets out of it again. People love that story!"

The great mythologist Joseph Campbell, whose Hero's Journey has informed the work of so many great writers and filmmakers, including George Lucas of *Star Wars* fame, broke the stories of the world's great myths into three main segments: Separation, Initiation, and Return. Beginning, middle, and end.

But while the Hero's Journey was considerably more complex than Vonnegut's summary—it included seventeen phases—the essence is similar. The hero is called to adventure, resists it, and sets out. Along the way, he or she faces great challenges, meets mentors, captures the prize, and returns back home. Upon the return, while many things seem similar, so much has changed.

Sound familiar? Someone gets into trouble and gets out of it again. Trouble leads to transformation.

People love that story!

And while the Hero's Journey certainly informs this book, the structure of great myths can be overwhelming as we shape and deliver our own most valuable insights. So in the following chapters, I will work with you on a distilled framework that you can use when considering any story.

One significant reference point comes in the story work done by Pixar. In her viral compilation called *22 Rules of Storytelling*,[12] Pixar storyboard artist Emma Coats listed out a storytelling frame used by the studio's writers to help inform their scripts. It went like this:

Once upon a time, _____.
Every day, _____.
One day, _____.
Because of that, _____.
And because of that, _____.
Until finally, _____.

This frame, sometimes called the Story Spine, predates Pixar. It is often credited to playwright Kenn Adams, and has long been used as a series of prompts in improvisational comedy skits. Sometimes there's another line added, to make it a seven-step structure:

And ever since then, _____.

This helps to clarify the beats of almost any story. For example:

Once upon a time, the Prince finished his training with the master and received five weapons along with a new name: Prince Five-Weapons.

Every day, he headed home past villages in the countryside.

And then one day, while walking through the forest, a great ogre called Sticky-Hair threatened to kill him.

Because of that, Prince Five-Weapons fought back with his weapons, but was stuck in the ogre's hair.

And because of that, he threw his body at Sticky-Hair, but then he became stuck in the ogre's hair.

Until finally, he had an insight to tell Sticky-Hair about the thunderbolt in his belly, and the ogre let the prince go.

And ever since then, Sticky-Hair has become as kind as an ogre can be. And the prince went on to become one of the incarnations of the Buddha.

I've used the Story Spine to help craft many stories over the years. Distilling further, and layering in the teachings of other story experts, we can draw out signposts that will help you shape your most essential insights into memorable, retellable stories.

THE JOURNEY CURVE

If there's one ingredient to every good story, it's this:

And no change, no story.

Without change you're more likely to describe an experience without conclusion, a ramble without an end, or a series of data points that few will remember. But with a purposeful and patient change, shown across time and space, you connect us to the act of getting into trouble, and getting out of it again.

Delta. Transformation. Twist. Whatever name you use, change is the catalytic element that makes a retelling so worthwhile. Change is woven into a story's DNA: it brings to life the trials and the triumphs, and makes the resulting lessons more memorable.

A retellable story needs change to move the story forward, to keep audiences attentive as they try to anticipate the course, and to build to a good payoff. It illuminates the *uh-ohs* at the beginning, the *a-has* in the middle, and the ahhhs at the end, and puts a pleasing end to the audience's hidden guesses.

Each change—or story pivot—reinforces the greater journey of the story, and held together they are the key elements of the universal story framework I will refer to throughout this book. It's called the Journey Curve.

The Journey Curve is a story guide, revealing where a story comes to life and what's missing. The Journey Curve draws from Vonnegut, Campbell, and the Story Spine to illuminate the primary pivots of any story. In order to get to the center of your stories you'll need not twenty pivots or ten, but just three:

1. *And then one day*
2. *Until finally*
3. *Ever since then*

Workshop your story with these key changes, and you'll build a better, more memorable story.

Here is a Journey Curve mapping the Prince Five-Weapons story.

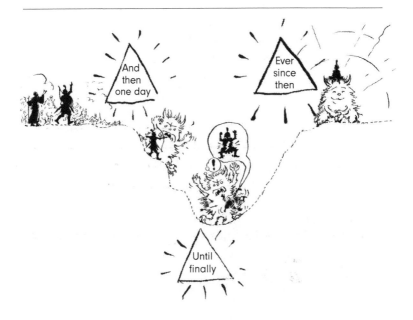

And then one day takes us from the beginning—the *once upon a time* world, where the Prince had completed his studies—and brings us to a key moment that sparks a journey of discovery. That key moment, in this case, is when the Prince meets the ogre. *Until finally* shifts us from the depths of trial—the most essential moment when the Prince is stuck in the ogre's hair, and he speaks of the thunderbolt in his belly—and propels us into the world of possibility. *Ever since then* takes us through the last challenges, and anchors the change, revealing how the world is now: Because of this interaction with the Prince, the ogre becomes a friend to the people of the village.

There are many ways to use the Journey Curve, and we'll get to these in the subsequent sections. In some instances, your curve may begin with just a few ideas mapped out. The process may begin with just an inkling of the point of the story, or with just one key pivot, or maybe the *until finally* moment is the only thing that's clear. Or it may begin with a list of story beats, leaving the decisions on the key moments for later.

As far as form goes, there's no artistry required! Images can simply help remind you about the key moments. You may choose to use words only, or stick figures, or both.

Using the Journey Curve means honing the change first and foremost, creating emblematic moments anchored in time and space, bringing them to life with the senses, and taking us through a challenge to a satisfying and relevant conclusion.

Let's zoom in a bit more.

Viet Nam protestor... loved country wanted to serve

USING THE PIVOTS

To take your audience members on a journey, you need to lead them out of the room to another place and time. If you take them with purpose, they can't help but go with you. And so a story begins by transporting your audience to another place and time, hence the phrase *once upon a time*.

A pivot means something only if we understand how the world was before, and contrast is often our greatest ally in a story. So use it! Draw us into the scene: What it was like there, who was there, and what their lives were like every day. Just a few details will do. *Every day, I'd go for a slow walk with my grandfather through the tree-lined park.* Two or three details surrounding each key moment will be enough to draw us in.

You may, of course, bristle at the storybook language. So try a more modern version of *once upon a time*: "Five years ago, when I was thirty." Or "Last week I was walking down the street . . ." Or you may choose to use once upon a time in a way that's more tongue-in-cheek. But use it! It will make your impending pivot that much more rewarding.

Pivot # 1: And Then One Day

If there were a contest for the most popular phrase in retellable stories, *and then one day* would win hands down. In movies, in conversations, in communications, as the scene builds, we know the *and then one day is* coming—or, shall I say, we hope it is coming—this magical turn of events that reminds us of the surprises that the world has in store.

When *and then one day* shows up in the room, you know you're in a story. Ears perk up. Something's *happening*.

I have a client, Maddy Dychtwald, an author, keynote speaker and expert on the changing face of retirement. To illuminate the concept that our idea of *old* has changed, she tells the story of Ida Keeling, a woman who in her sixties was so distraught over losing both her sons that she barely left the house.

*And then one da*y, Ida's daughter, Shelley, got her up from the couch and walking around the house. Some time later, Shelley came back and prompted her mom to walk around the block. Two years later, Shelley signed her up for a 5K race.

This year, the great-great-grandmother from New York City set a world record in the 100-meter race in her age bracket, at the ripe young age of one hundred.

*And then one da*y illuminates the initial change of state. It is also a great way to let your audience know that you are in control of the story. And the sense of controlling the story is very valuable for a storyteller. Control is different than memorization. You're driving!

Control means knowing the journey ahead, and taking us there.

And then one day the phone rang. However, there was a problem . . .

And then one day I picked up the paper. There, on the front page . . .

And then one day carries a story into the phase of discovery and trial, into a new world where different things are possible, and challenges you never imagined appeared, and were faced. As you face them, you dive deeper into the minds and hearts of your audiences.

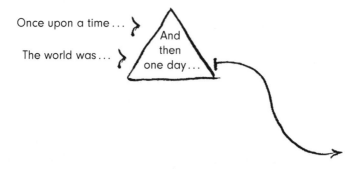

It's helpful to build confidence as you tell your story, as well. Even if you're telling a story you've never told before, if you know you've got an *and then one day* out in front of you, it will help you guide the story.

It may be very hard to choose a moment for your story. Don't worry about the perfect moment at first; try to find one emblematic moment that informs the turn, or simply one that you can feel . . .

Grandma falls ill. The bottom drops out of the market. The Cossacks arrive. The tension increases, and we begin to guess what's going to happen.

Stories don't all require a journey into the depths. Sometimes, the change is much more simple. Sometimes *and then one day* is enough to depict a change.

But sometimes it's not. Sometimes, the journey goes on, and the audience asks: And then what happened?

"Okay, enough already! I'll do it!" says the hero. She buys the plane ticket. He goes to a strange city looking for a pilot. She refuses to give up her seat on the bus.

The journey has begun.

Pivot #2: Until Finally

The Journey Curve takes us on a voyage. From the *and then one day*, we drop into the problem, into challenge, and into discovery.

A story, at its essence, is about somebody who wants something and can't have it. So as you draw us into the story's challenge, we begin to see how one thing led to the next, experiencing the small (or large) shifts along the way. Cause and effect becomes clear, and the tension increases.

Because of that, he used all of his weapons. And because of that, he got stuck in the hair.

Because of that, and that, and that. *Because of that* is a convention that helps us progress in the story, listing actions without having to list every single detail. It's a fairly efficient way of sharing a lot of information tucked into the story that might spread over days or months, or just a few hours.

And so we slide deeper down the Journey Curve, into the gulley. The gulley is where things get harder. Into trouble, out of trouble, and maybe into it again.

Not every story plunges to the depths. Not every story involves someone getting stuck deep down in what Joseph Campbell called *the belly of the whale*. But some do. And most others can benefit from drawing a moment or two from the real feeling of trial.

In his book *The Writer's Journey*, Christopher Vogler called this phase the *inmost cave*.[13] Here at the lowest point of the story, the journey may seem like a very bad idea. Here, one may think things can't get any worse—but they still do. Strength is tested, and resilience is built.

In the inmost cave, also called the innermost cave, you don't seem to have the power, the support, or the will to create the change that is needed.

Here, everything seems to be going against the hero. This is the hardest moment, the loneliest moment. The tears, the fears, the heartbreak. In *Star Wars*, Luke gets sucked underwater by a one-eyed serpent in the Death Star's great garbage compactor. He finally comes up gasping for air . . . and then the walls of the trash smasher start moving in.

Dang. It just keeps getting harder!

The innermost cave may have lasted an hour, a day, or a year. But it can be represented in one emblematic moment. Walking the streets in despair, rustling through the sock drawer for food money. Will the funder come? Will the community rally? Cortisol release. Pay attention!

In that moment, as the audience, we don't know. Hope is dim.

But, you know, enough is enough. They have to get out of the gulley. Change . . . or die.

That's the power of *until finally*. The journey seems all but lost, when suddenly you remember something your mentor once told you, or find something that you were given long ago that helps you out. You muster the strength, as a person or group, to step beyond what was once thought possible.

This change may happen because, well, you just can't take any more. You realize you're headed in a direction that really needs to shift. Maybe you find the key (or the strength or the power) that you realize you had all along.

Or maybe you really see what the future looks like if you stay on your current path—and you don't like it at all.

Until finally, something changed. Until finally, the phone rang. Until finally, the doctor said I could go home. Until finally, R2D2 plugged into the Death Star mainframe and shut down the trash masher.

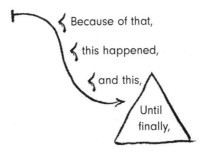

However it happened, something transformed. A new strength has been realized. And from this moment something new begins to emerge. The change of the story itself may be embodied in this one turn.

Because you've built the tension, and the curiosity, the *until finally* moment may be the one your audience will remember above all else. It's the key twist in the tale.

When you emerge from the *until finally* moment, the world is already different. You've begun to come out on the other side. It might be some change in you, or some change in the world around you, but regardless, a distinct change has occurred.

But you're not yet done; you still have to climb your way out.

Pivot #3: Ever Since Then

Ever since then reveals the final and lasting change that anchors the new world that you have entered. It grounds the change.

There may be a few steps that you take to truly emerge on the other side of the story. You may have one last trial that threatens to put you back in the innermost cave. Or perhaps just another step along the way of your growth; another job or a series of projects that brought you to the present moment.

But the fact is, the journey is easier now. The ice has melted; it's springtime. You've learned. The old challenges, pains, or temptations have lost their pull.

Eventually, you emerge to tell the story. You've gotten into trouble, and you've gotten out of trouble. The change that your story reveals is sometimes a subtle, simple lesson that rounds out your journey and depicts your future course. And while there may be many similarities to the old world, this world is also very new. It's different—and you are different, either inside or out.

Ever since then, I always look both ways before crossing the street. Ever since then, I have dedicated myself to maintaining the health of my local community.

Ever since then may be a surprise, or the clear illumination of a lesson—or it may simply provide deeper meaning to what we know about you already. *And that's why we . . .*

Looking back to the beginning of your story, to your *once upon a time*, and comparing it to your *ever since then*, there is a clear and distinct change. Back then, you may have believed something entirely different. Or, let's admit it, maybe you saw the world in a slightly naïve way.

Ever since then is a chance to land the message of your story. It may be a humble dedication or a bold vision, or it may be both. You may have averted disaster, or fallen into it and emerged with a lesson. You may be left with a simple conclusion, one that may shift slightly based on the purpose of the story, and the audience. But however it's told, one thing is clear: You got into trouble, and . . . you got out of trouble. People love that story!

Ever since then, we've been working on a battery that would solve the energy crisis . . .

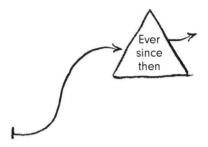

Find these pivots, and you find your story. Find your story, and you reveal who you are, what you do, and why you do it.

The Curve can help you map any journey. But it is the guide, not the rule. Anecdotes may have a quick *and then one day*, and that's it. Funny stories may be a quick dip into the gulley and then end with an unexpected twist. But while you may not always use every step of the Curve, you can always draw on one, two, or three changes to help you increase your retellability. You can always consider where you are on the Journey Curve, and what may be needed.

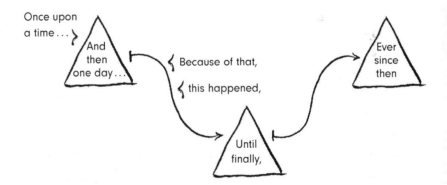

As you practice your framing, your stories will become more natural. Your story gathering will be more efficient as you begin to recognize key pivots; your shaping will be more effective;

and, as you'll more intimately understand the beats of your story, you'll be less at risk of a misstep while presenting. Thus, you may well be able to be more present to the audience and to emerging ideas while you tell your story.

But don't take my word for it . . . yet. Let's put the model to work in a few story scenarios.

There are three kinds of stories: those that tell where you come from, those that say where you are today, and those that reveal where you are going. Know these, and you will know your journey.

Chapter 4

THREE KINDS OF STORIES

Experience. Origin Stories.
Impact Stories. Vision Stories.

EXPERIENCE

Nasrudin is known as much for his wisdom as for his foolishness, and many are those who have sought out his teaching.

One devotee tracked him down for many years before finding him in the marketplace sitting atop a pile of banana peels—no one knows why.

"Oh great sage, Nasrudin," said the eager student. "I must ask you a very important question, the answer to which we all seek: What is the secret to attaining happiness?"

Nasrudin thought for a time, then responded.

"The secret of happiness is good judgment."

"Ah," said the student. "But how do we attain good judgment?"

"From experience," answered Nasrudin.

"Yes," said the student. "But how do we attain experience?"

"Bad judgment."

—Joel ben Izzy, The Beggar King and the Secret of Happiness

Ah, happiness. Success. Accomplishment. How much the heart yearns for such transformation! And yet, there is always a price to pay, and a challenge to be had. As the trickster Nasrudin reveals, that path to happiness is lined with unexpected hurdles, sudden insights, and, well, bad judgment. This is how new things emerge, and how experiences become assets: You try, you fail, you orient yourself, and you learn something.

Journeys that move predictably from point A to point B don't seem to have the same impact: the mishaps and surprises make the stories much more satisfying. Perhaps, as mythologist Michael Meade once said, it is because "The soul wants an outer drama to match its mythic interior."

And while we have many bits of stories in a variety of forms, there are three main genres of stories: Those that tell us where we come from, those that tell us what we do now, and those that tell us where we're going.

Origin stories, impact stories, and vision stories.

In this chapter, we'll take a step deeper into story shaping, applying the Journey Curve, and exploring stories that are at once very personal and also essential to your professional journey.

We'll start with where you come from.

ORIGIN STORIES

Of the three main genres of leadership stories, origin stories are often the most retellable. Why? In part, because they are the most likely to involve some clear action and some clear change of state. And also because they're likely the most practiced.

Origin stories depict your beginnings. They hold your DNA, revealing key moments of insight and early influences that help us understand who you are today, without having to know every single hurdle you've ever overcome. You may have several of them: why you do the work you do; why you came to this particular phase of work; why you are passionate about some particular obscure thing; or how your company began. They may show up on your website, in your TED Talk, in your bio, and they may also inform your elevator story—your career "why" story told in its most distilled form (see chapter 7).

Sometimes origins tap into the humility of beginnings. A couple of friends named Bill and Dave were hard at work in a garage in Palo Alto in 1938, inventing what they called an "audio oscillator," a mechanism that generated one pure sound at a time. A sound engineer from a Hollywood film studio sensed it would do the trick to address some complicated audio needs for their upcoming film *Fantasia*. Disney asked for a few modifications and ordered eight of them for $71.50 each.[14]

That was the beginning of Hewlett-Packard.

Sometimes a key ally or mentor arrives just at the right time. The American naturalist John Muir, with his long white beard, heavy wool coat, and a chunk of bread in his pocket, looked out across Yosemite with a young politician named Teddy Roosevelt. The two had camped near Glacier Point and had awoken to five inches of fresh snow, which delighted Roosevelt. Muir spoke to him of the problems in protecting the region, and they discussed the future of the park.

That camping trip is considered the beginning of Yosemite National Park, and the catalyst that led to Roosevelt's protection of over 100 million acres of national forests.[15]

Origin stories have many benefits:

- They reveal to customers, partners, and funders why you do your work in the world—and why that work matters.
- They show what you've learned on your journeys, and

how much you've grown.
- They help win a job or a client.
- They create connection among team members around a common goal or through a transition.
- They lend strength and meaning to your mission.

These stories appear every day—on the backs of yogurt containers, on radio shows, and at the doors of restaurants.

Sometimes origin stories reveal a burning question that gives life to an opportunity. Such is the case with one certain brother and sister who took a trip with their family to the Grand Canyon in late 1999. Ahmed, a filmmaker who had been living in Europe, and Reem, a painter, stood on the rim of the canyon, talking about the individual journeys that had taken them around the world to Europe, to Africa, and to their family's native Iraq. Reem brought up a topic that was frequently discussed at family gatherings: Who was going to bring back the tea, called *numi*, made from the dry lime that grows in the Middle Eastern desert?

"I've decided I want to do it," said Reem as they walked on the canyon's edge.

"So do I!" said her brother.

With that conversation, a tea company was born. Reem's original paintings became the first packaging art, and she became their first creative director. Ahmed, who ran teahouses in Prague, became the CEO, head of sales, and the alchemist who mixed their signature blends. Now, seventeen years later, Numi is available in fifty-five countries and is the largest organic fair-trade tea company in America. Numi's origin story infuses everything they do, from a respect for global cultures, to a dedication to fair compensation for farmers around the world, to how they name and design an ever-growing line of unique teas.

When setting out to create your own origin story, there can

be many beginnings from which to choose, and many questions. Do you, for example, begin with your first job, the moment your founders first met, or the wisdom you gained from your grandma? Do you start with the problem, or the way the world was before? Experimentation will tell: each question may serve to inform a different aspect of why you do the work you do, lay out the purpose of your company, or simply serve to explain a bit more about what guides you. So you may end up with several stories—or several versions of the same story, each of which may be applied differently for different audiences.

Origin stories aren't only about companies, of course. They happen all the time! Origins can be the beginning of anything. They tell your motivations (why you do what you do), and reveal enough of your greater journey to put the rest in context. Maybe you had an a-ha moment or a turnaround that changed the course of your life. Maybe you're telling the story of why a particular product was created. Or you've got a story of when you just got fed up, and began a new adventure.

Origin stories are much easier to remember than mission statements, and they can be told much more naturally and personally.

"The story must explain at a fundamental level why you exist," says Ben Horowitz, cofounder of the venture capital firm Andreessen Horowitz. "Why does the world need your company? Why do we need to be doing what we're doing, and why is it important?"[16]

You don't have to *tell* your origin story on your site, or on your packaging, or in your keynotes. But as a leader, you should know it, and know it well. Part of the value of going back and doing some excavation is that this work goes a long way to providing an understanding of the future—for yourself, for those around you, and for your audiences.

This is especially true when offerings have evolved; when you are in transition; when you're creating your mission, vision, and values; when you've grown from five to fifty; on a particular anniversary; or when a founder has moved on.

Since the Journey Curve is a vehicle of change, it's critical that you know the change that you're depicting: that is, how the world was before your origin, and how it is now. And of course this is largely dependent on your audience, and the point you have in telling the story.

Sometimes origin stories depict innovation born from frustration. One such story begins in 1990, near the end of a 175-mile bike ride. Still far from home, Gary Erikson was bonking—that is, tapped out of energy. He needed fuel to keep riding, but all he had was the last of six of those rubbery-tasting energy bars that dominated the market at the time. But Gary just couldn't eat one more of them. "I think I can make something better than this," he said to his riding buddy in a moment of hunger and frustration.

This wasn't a passing idea. Gary owned a small bakery, and upon his return, he got to work. After nearly two years of experimenting with flavors and packaging in his mother's kitchen, he came up with a bar that would change the industry. It would also help many others feel a sense of power and enjoyment during the most challenging moments of their most difficult adventures. Gary named the bar after his dad—calling it Clif Bar—and the wrapper depicted a climber deftly powering up a steep cliff.

Innovation is sometimes born from one key moment. And this particular moment on a long bike ride sparked a story that is still being told today in a thousand different ways. The story comes to life at the Clif Bar headquarters, where organic food is served, yoga classes run nonstop, and commuter bikes fill the entryway. The story is also ritualized in an annual "Epiphany Ride," a daylong employee ride that connects employees both to the beginnings of the company and to the daily experience of the customers they serve.

Taking the Clif Bar story into the Journey Curve, the pivots can be clearly mapped. In this case, there was a distinct *and then one day*: the bike ride.

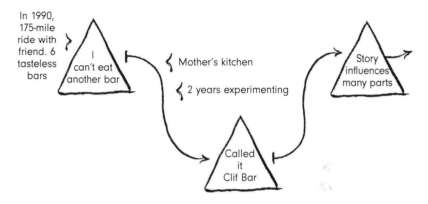

Note this: The *until finally* moment may not be the launch, or the name of the bar. It may be the first trade show, the first year of sales, or even the moment years later when Gary shook off an offer to be acquired, became saddled with millions of dollars in debt, and Clif Bar stayed independent. The *until finally* moment—and any of the moments in the Journey Curve—can be turned and shifted depending on your audience and the objectives of your story. Because, of course, not all of us have an epiphany around which to pivot.

It may be difficult at first to find a viable emblematic moment that fits into an *and then one day* or an *until finally*. So my suggestion is to come up with a few options, and try them out. Time and practice will tell.

IMPACT STORIES

While origin stories help you draw from the road you've traveled, impact stories represent the ground under your feet. They reveal *what you do now.* Impact stories illuminate key moments in your work, define your offering, and put a face on the changes you've helped catalyze.

The impacts are there; sometimes it's just a matter of discovering them and shaping them.

A couple of years ago, I was working with the customer support team of a global video site. The purpose of the story training was to build capacity, connection, and a sense of personal respect both inside the team—among those who are responsible to protect and serve the global user community—and across the larger company. This was because, as it turned out, most of the attention and resources in the company went to the big distribution projects and sponsors, leaving less attention for the group that helped the customers succeed.

At one point during the session, a manager shared a story about a young woman in Australia who threatened suicide and posted a video about it. In the past, if such information was shared, it might raise alerts with the school, or with friends, or a therapist. But in the modern day, when communications can happen within a global, decentralized community, the response is different.

This site and many other global sites rely on a community-based flagging system to identify things that people see as problematic. The challenge with such a system—at a global scale—is that there may be twenty thousand flags a day. Thousands of people may flag a Justin Bieber video as inappropriate because they dislike it. Determining the truly risky ones is key. So the site relies on a balance between machine learning and community indicators.

In this case, the girl's video was flagged by an attentive community member on the other side of the world, in Spain. It was quickly identified in Dublin, Ireland as a real issue and sent to California, where someone notified the police in Queensland. As a result, the Queensland Royal Police showed up at the girl's home within a few hours of the original posting, and danger was averted—the girl's parents hadn't even known there was a problem.

As a dad, this story struck me as both terrifying and fascinating. Imagine you're a parent sitting upstairs and you don't even know what your child is going through because the conversation isn't with a counselor—it's with the world.

This became an important impact story that the leaders could use to give meaning to the work they do every day—both to one another, and to the leaders of the parent company.

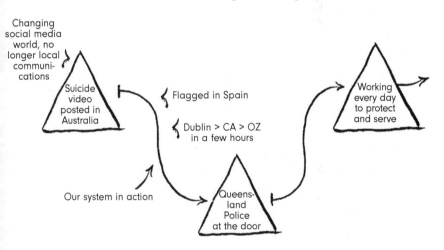

Impact stories may embody your values, the key attributes of your product, or your particular approach to making an impact in the world.

Sometimes impact stories may seem to parallel your origin story. At other times your customers may find the same challenge you once found, and your story illuminates that parallel. But it doesn't mean you—or your organization or product—are the hero of your own story. As my friend Jonah Sachs says in his exploration into modern mythmaking called *Story Wars*,[17] your company or product may be better served to represent the mentor—or helper—rather than the hero.

In the Journey Curve above, the story shows a teller who aspires to provide its emerging global community with the tools to communicate with one another—and also to help one other. Here the community is the hero; the teller is the helper.

Gary Erickson's story has sparked hundreds of other stories that have presented Clif Bar as the helper, whether speaking to the mountain climber facing the last pitch up Yosemite's Half Dome or the runner finishing her first 10k. *We're not the hero; you are. We just lend a hand at the right time.*

Sometimes impact stories are called *success stories* or *case studies*. But of course, going too quickly to the success can drain the power out of the story. And a case study often skips the most memorable part of the challenge: the bumps along the way that bring the accomplishment to life.

Impact stories are often about one person and how his life was changed as a result of your work. The stories introduce us to the main character—your customer, partner, or a public citizen—and the problem she faced. They show how you (or your collaborators, or your product) played a role in addressing the problem. Well-delivered, impact stories can depict a transformation, reveal essential data points, and land a key message.

Maybe you're a teacher, and you see how an interventional reading program has helped a student learn to love books. Maybe you're a dentist wishing to convey the dangers of neglecting a cavity. Or perhaps you've helped transform a neighborhood or helped bring a company from the edge of disaster into a thriving enterprise.

Some of the most familiar impact stories are TV commercials.

They may not be stories of real people, of course; rather, they are little depictions of change that relate to a bigger story. "Before, my clothes were always brown. Now, they're glistening white!" One of my childhood favorites is about a kid name Mikey. Two kids won't eat their cereal. So they pass it to their brother Mikey, who will never eat anything. But to their surprise, he starts eating it. And he likes it. "He likes it! Hey Mikey!"

There is no Mikey, of course, at least not one that I know of—but there are also many fussy-eating Mikeys. I share this to say that in a story, the personal can become universal. One person facing one problem, told in a meaningful way, can create a powerful affinity to a person, to a brand, or to a movement.

Impact stories may be told at a dinner party or a presentation, or used to give an example of your work through video, social media, or blogs. So having an available collection of *go-to* impact stories that you can map to particular purposes and particular audiences will make your daily story delivery much more fun and useful.

A well-told impact story can help:

- Remind you and those around you why you do this work.
- Inform decisions going forward and raise money.
- Show that your funds have been well allocated.
- Recruit.
- Sell.
- Build community.

Impact stories, whether through the difficult stories of individuals facing hardship or the simple act of describing a potential customer experience, are a way of giving meaning to numbers and physical changes in the world. They are the cousins of case studies, which lack the suspense and curiosity of good stories, and are rarely retold.

VISION STORIES

Vision stories tell us where you're going. They draw your audience into the future, pulling them into the journey, rallying their participation in making a great shift.

In their most simple form, vision stories can be origin stories building to a vision statement: "And that's why, today, our vision is . . ." Your audience, or your team, may never repeat a vision statement without sounding robotic and memorized, but your vision stories are another matter.

Standing in front of the Lincoln Memorial on a hot day in August of 1963, Martin Luther King didn't deliver a one-sentence, distilled vision statement. He took us to another future. He illuminated the challenges of today as he reached into tomorrow.

I have a dream that one day on the red hills of Georgia the sons of former slaves and the sons of former slave owners will be able to sit down together at the table of brotherhood.

I have a dream that one day even the state of Mississippi, a state sweltering with the heat of injustice, sweltering with the heat of oppression, will be transformed into an oasis of freedom and justice.[18]

Every one of those 250,000 in attendance, and those millions that have seen the speech on TV or heard it on the radio, became a part of a journey. And the transformation continues today.

A vision story creates the contrast between how the world is now and how it will be. Because while contrast is a key ally in any story, it has a distinct role in a vision story: contrast helps build the tension that lets everyone around you find her or his place in the unfolding future.

I have a dream that my four little children will one day live in a nation where they will not be judged by the color of their skin but by the content of their character.

A well-told vision story can help you:

- Navigate changing seas.
- Raise money.
- Motivate, inspire, and guide your audience.
- Change the future.

Vision stories bring a pivot into focus for those around you—and that pivot may be today. Take for example the Elon Musk story depicted earlier—the smokestacks he featured are billowing right now, and the batteries are hooked up to solar panels right now. A new future unfolds, and a vision becomes reality.

In October 1983, Steve Jobs stood in front of a packed auditorium to speak about the upcoming release of the new Macintosh.

He could have just delivered his message:

Apple is the future.

But he didn't. A story is a journey, and Jobs knew that. And an explanation, or a detailing of the facts, is not a journey. An explanation sparks neither curiosity nor inspiration.

He could have just blamed his adversary:

IBM is Big Brother.

But he didn't do that either, because blame can backfire. And it can motivate people only so far. Jobs told a story, and landed with a burning question.

It is 1958. IBM passes up the chance to buy a fledgling company that has just invented a new technology called Xerography. Two years later Xerox is born and IBM has been kicking itself ever since. It is ten years later, the late '60s. Digital Equipment and others invent the mini computer. IBM dismisses the mini computer as too small to do serious computing and therefore unimportant to its business . . .

It is now ten years later, the late '70s. In 1977, Apple, a young fledgling company on the West Coast, invents the Apple II, the first personal computer as we know it today. IBM dismisses the personal computer as too small to do serious computing and unimportant to its business . . .

It is now 1984. It appears IBM wants it all. Apple is perceived to be the only hope to offer IBM a run for its money. Dealers, initially welcoming IBM with open arms, now fear an IBM-dominated and controlled future. They are increasingly turning back to Apple as the only force that can ensure their future freedom!

IBM is aiming its guns toward the last obstacle to industry control—Apple. Will Big Blue dominate the entire computer industry? The entire Information Age?

Was George Orwell right about 1984?[19]

This key question illuminated a fork in road: Do you want a colorless Big Brother future or a future infused with creativity and innovation? The question was pounded home by the Ridley Scott–directed commercial that followed, featuring a sleek Olympian athlete chased by storm trooper-like forces while she's running through a room of gray shaved-headed masses entranced by Big Brother on an enormous screen. She throws her hammer to smash the screen, and a new future is unleashed.

"On January 24th, Apple Computer will introduce Macintosh. And you'll see why 1984 won't be like *Nineteen Eighty-Four.*"

Of course, it's a false choice—who wants *that* 1984? But the speech and the commercial framed the conversation. Especially to his audience of the day—750 sales reps for whom the future was really on the line. They got the point: *the moment to act is right now.*

You may not have Steve Jobs' knack for speaking—not many do. And you may not have suitcases of cash to create the next great ad campaign. But you do have the ability to draw your audience into a key moment of change and show the difference between how the world was and how it can be. (is)

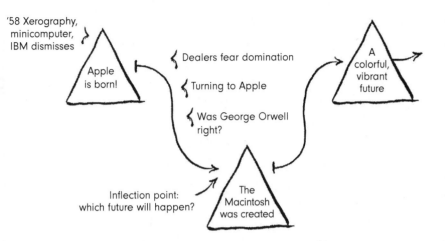

Your vision story might just turn the tide or help a team member to act boldly—today, tomorrow, or in the distant future. It all depends on the purpose, the audience, and the ability to find the right story.

Your life has been woven with so many surprises. So many lessons that can benefit others. So many insights. So many moments. Some, you've revealed in the stories you tell today. But many others will be revealed in the stories you tell tomorrow.

Chapter 5

BUILD YOUR COLLECTION OF STORIES

What to Do with Fruit. Prepare Your Repertoire. Gather Your Go-Tos. Refine Your Reserves. Discover Losses and Lessons. Arrange Your Loose Change. The Might of Insight. Suggestion: A Story Box.

WHAT TO DO WITH FRUIT

Three men came from different lands where there was no fruit. Having learned of the location of a thing called a fruit tree, each traveled far to find out for himself.

The first, with his head buried in his map, walked right past the tree and never found it. "There is no such thing as fruit!" he said.

The second found the tree, but discovered to his dismay that the fruit was overripe. "I hate rotten things." And he began the long trip back home, disappointed with this thing called fruit.

The third found the tree and saw that much of the fruit had gone bad. He sat there for a long time, holding the soft fruit in his hand, thinking very deeply about what to do with this. Opening the fruit to the center, he found a pit. And finding that the pit was a seed, he realized that all he had to do was put it in the ground, water it, and wait.

—Adapted from Tahir Shaw, *In Arabian Nights*

A story is like a seed. Undoubtedly there are times you will be too busy or tied up in directives or messages to feel the richness of a story, and you'll walk right on past. Other times a story may seem overripe or overused.

The stories you tell depend on the challenges you find around you. Perhaps, you'll find, a team member is dejected after losing a big project. One of your stories might reveal a project that you lost and what you learned from it. Maybe your customers seem to have the same contention again and again, and you reveal a story of a similar customer with a similar challenge. Maybe you're speaking at an all-hands staff meeting about a big strategic shift that will take some compromises, and you have a story that reveals the power of acting quickly.

In the next chapter we'll explore how to build a collection of stories. That is, how to find them, shape them, and practice them.

PREPARE YOUR REPERTOIRE

I used to believe that when it comes to telling stories, you've either "got it" or you don't. But after many years of helping clients face all kinds of hurdles with their storytelling—from a discomfort with the spotlight, to the tendency to move too quickly through the story, to a wariness of vulnerability, to the challenge of finding a message and getting the ending right —I no longer feel that way.

After trying and testing my own story practice, and training hundreds of leaders from many countries, I believe that everyone can tell good stories. And you don't need long-term coaching to do it; commitment to listening and practice is the price of entry.

And so, since you've made it this far into the book, consider this challenge. Your mission, should you choose to accept it, is to find, shape, and share five retellable stories. That is, a collection of stories from which you can pull, for a variety of purposes, for a variety of audiences.

Perhaps it will take you a short time to collect the lessons, insights, challenges, and changes that give form to your stories. Perhaps it will take you a month. Or a year. But however long it takes to start the engine, the journey is worth it.

Why five? Because it's a good start. It's enough to create diversity in your telling. Of course, you may have more, or you may be very satisfied with three.

Building your repertoire requires you to scan your life and your leadership, gather your experiences, and see how they map to your critical messages and audiences. To help you, I've broken down the stories into categories:

- Your *go-tos*, which you already know and tell, but can always use refinement;
- Your *reserves*, which are almost ready to go, but not quite;
- Your *losses and lessons*, struggles and challenges that don't yet make retellable stories for one reason or another;
- Your *loose change*, a collection of twists and turns in your life that you haven't yet formed into stories;
- And finally, your *insights*, those momentary sparks that inform where your life leads, that may pull at you from time to time, saying, "Hey! Think about this!"

My hope is that the suggestions above will help you freshen up the stories you already love to tell and give you new perspectives on how to begin them, how to anchor them, how to play with the audience as you deepen them, and how to land them. Once shaped, they can be used for a variety of purposes: to inform your career, your marketing, your presentations, your strategies, and your management.

Take these suggestions with a grain of salt. They are guidelines, and in the end everyone finds stories differently. Trust your instincts and what your own rich experiences reveal.

GATHER YOUR GO-TOS

Your *go-to* stories are ones you may already tell, but could still use some work. They may be stories you share at dinner parties, at interviews, on the big stage, or even that one story you tell about growing up. Your *go-tos* might also be stories that you have written but have never told live. You may never have thought much about them or how they might be shared in more diverse ways. Yet these stories can always be reshaped, improved, or guided differently.

One story might depict your origins, showing a moment where something began, where you come from, or how you discovered your passion or your career. One might be something funny that happened once, something that taught you about how the world works. Another might be an *a-ha* moment, a key insight that turns the course of your adventures. Yet another might be a unique experience that is relevant to a frequent business challenge, or an emblematic moment that represents a certain customer's problem. You may find a few that are about mistakes made and lessons that you find worth sharing.

Last but not least, one *go-to* may be your *core story*, the story that holds all the rest, telling what you do and where you're going.

To get a handle on your *go-tos*, ask yourself a few questions about the stories you already tell. Which ones are they? How often do you tell them?

Taking each story, consider these questions:

- What's working with the story?
- Does it drop into the suspense and the surprise, and land a key insight?
- Is there a place where people usually respond?
- What's the change in your story? Do you begin with the world looking a certain way and end with it seeming a different way?
- Do you depict at least one scene or place in the story where the senses come alive?
- What is your one key takeaway or message?
- Does your story tell a bit too much all at the beginning, leaving a slightly flat ending—or just wander on with no certain end point?
- How long is your story? Do you have a couple of versions—a three-minute version and a thirty-second version? (See more in chapter 7)
- And finally, here's an important one: Why do you tell it? (Why do you care, and why should others care?)

Often, when we take a closer look at our stories, we realize they can feel forced or stagnant. Don't worry if you've told these stories many times—as you give them more attention, they will change and improve, becoming more relevant to a variety of purposes. Some of your friends or associates may have heard a story before—they may even say, "I've heard this before." But they're talking about the old version; they may be pleasantly surprised by the way you tell it now.

Resist the temptation to bury your well-worn stories and your difficult experiences. Rather, use the tools and techniques I offer in the following chapters to rework them and give them a new beginning, a new end, or a new connection to the lesson of the moment.

Some examples of *go-to* stories:

- The day you realized this was the job for you
- A "satisfied customer" impact story
- A "why you left that last job" story
- A story that tells us what innovation looks like
- A story about a famous person whose work you respect
- One metaphor or folktale that reinforces messages you find yourself repeating

REFINE YOUR RESERVES

Reserves are stories you may know but haven't been ready to tell.

When I was in my twenties, working my way through a year in France, I spent one weekend helping out a farmer named Alan. Our first job was to empty out a horse stable that was a foot deep in manure. After a very long afternoon of shoveling and getting as dirty as was imaginable, we packed a surprising amount of the horse residue into bags and onto his horses and then walked alongside them six miles through the rocky, dusty mountain-scape. Finally, at nightfall, I arrived ragged and tired at one of the most beautiful vistas I have seen to this day: Alan's farm. Terraces upon terraces of flourishing greens and trees.

The next day, after rising with the sun to pick carrots, I made a joke to Alan about never having shoveled so much sh*t before. "*Sheed*?" he said in a heavy French accent, laughing. He pointed across his farm to his vast fields of greens, garlic, tomatoes, and apple trees. "That's not *sheed*. That's pure gold."

And so it is with your *reserves*. The power of your stories is often where you least expect it, hidden behind some trial or challenge or even something that stinks. Don't disregard the twists and turns and insights that guided you here just because they don't appear to be beautiful flowers right away. With some time, and some consideration of the issues and messages you're looking at now, your memories may have composted into something of great value.

Maybe it's a story you told once that didn't have the juice you wanted. Maybe it's something surprising that happened one time—a moment that just won't let you go—but doesn't seem quite like a story yet. Or it could be a story you read, or heard from someone else, one that could use some practice. Maybe you had a recent realization or an updated version of your origin story, but you don't like how it lands.

Your stories are not static or two-dimensional. Life has its way of flattening out memories, of making the extraordinary seem ordinary. In fact, as you begin to breathe life into your stories, you may find new elements you'd never noticed. Don't just think about it; go there in your imagination. One way to discover these, quite simply, is to give a listen to your life. Scan across the years, looking for curious situations that stick out. Bring your curiosity back to a certain moment, freezing it in time, to see what else is there. Just the act of trying on one emblematic moment that represents change gets you closer to a good story. Get curious! Can you smell the green grass of the field as you walked to your first meeting? Can you feel the soft rain on the roof or hear the knock at the door?

Is the takeaway what you once thought? Take a look at the list of story questions in the *go-to* section above and see what other shaping your *reserves* may need. You may even find that there are other lessons waiting for you.

Your *reserve* stories may be:

- Stories you've tried once or twice but never really landed
- Moments from your life or the lives of those around you that you'd like to retell
- Stories you've read or heard others tell
- Parables, folk stories, or metaphors

Your *reserves* provide a good opportunity to find a friend with whom you can practice: a story buddy. This is someone you can call up and safely tell an *in-the-works* story over the phone, over coffee, or even over voicemail, and get their feedback. More about this in Chapter 6.

If you're wondering if it's okay to retell someone else's story, and aren't sure, ask. If you don't know the teller, use your best judgment—if you wish, you can change the names of those involved. In general, just be respectful: As my friend Jed, an Internet strategist, says, "A story is like a car or a pet, so if you use someone else's, treat it nicely."

Take your *reserves* out for a ride. Get in the practice of hearing a story and retelling it, just for the exercise. Consider the questions above that help you refine your *go-tos*. Then try out these revised stories in a low-pressure environment: at a dinner party, with your friends, or in a meeting with a team member. With a niece or nephew.

Just remember: A story is a gift, so offer it with care.

DISCOVER LOSSES AND LESSONS

Some of our greatest leadership stories are formed from our "losses and lessons" stories, the falls and the failures that can become great allies we overlook in our search for stories. You may want to stuff them in the corner or push them into the past, thinking,

"Thankfully, I'm done with those times." But those trials and struggles—the stories that take us through the *innermost cave*—can be the best medicine for those around us who are facing relevant challenges of their own.

As the mythologist Michael Meade said in a lecture I attended, life isn't about avoiding trouble. It's about "getting into the right kind of trouble." The wrong kind of trouble can kill you. But the right kind of trouble gives you experience, a lesson, and a good story to pass on.

A couple of years ago, my son Izzy was having a rough baseball game. He had yelled from the dugout at the Little League umpire. Later, he seemed to want to argue with us about everything, and then he tripped his sister. "Go to your room!" I yelled, losing my cool. After a few minutes of realizing my own anger wasn't really helping the situation, I went in and climbed up next to him on his bunk bed, where he sat, head in hands.

"Iz. How do you feel about today's game?" I asked.

He looked up for a second. "It was terrible . . . We played terrible! I PLAYED TERRIBLE!"

My heart dropped. What do I say to that? I got quiet for a moment and cleared out of my mind whatever I thought was supposed to happen, any self-judgment, guilt, or anger that I had. I scanned my internal database to remember when I had been in a similar situation, to meet his challenge with one of my own.

I recalled a moment of deep frustration as a kid. Then I saw how it could be a story, with a beginning and an end.

But then I had to think for another long second to figure out how the story related.

"Did I ever tell you about the worst game I ever played?" Even as I said this, I was buying a little time, thinking about just how to share a failure that still rolls over in my mind, decades later.

"What happened?" he asked, looking up.

"I was seventeen. On the high school basketball team. It was a big night, because I knew I was finally breaking into the line-up. But then, I just made mistake after mistake. Missed an easy shot. A dumb foul. Threw the ball away. I was so frustrated, I even shoved a guy."

"Really?"

"Really. A very big guy. It got worse and worse. I've told you that your grandpa was a college coach—my life had been basketball since I was five years old. But my dream of being a star was fading quickly."

"And after that game, I got benched. For days afterward, sitting at the end of the bench, I was steaming mad. But really, I felt like I wanted to cry. Finally, I couldn't take any more, and I decided I would quit the very next day.

"But the next morning came, and I didn't quit."

"Why not?" my son asked.

"Because deep down inside, I knew that we had a very special team. And I wanted to be a part of it. So, instead of quitting, that morning I decided I had to put down my own dreams and put my energy into the team. So I started cheering more. I worked my butt off in practice, diving everywhere, playing crazy defense, working to help everyone get better. I still felt bad, but every time I'd feel bad about not playing, I'd refocus into the team. And do you know what happened?"

"What?" he asked, lifting up his head.

"We started to win. And I was hardly playing at all. We won the league, and then the county. It was like surfing a big wave. And I was able to enjoy it, to get out of the way and support the team."

"And you won the state, too, right?" He said, his reddened eyes starting to brighten.

"Right, we eventually won the state championship. And I

would roll in only at the end of games, when it was mostly decided. That was still hard! But every time I got frustrated, I put my focus back into the team."

He had forgotten about his frustration and was there with me, sitting on the sidelines in Oakland Arena at the state championship finals. And so, carefully, I worked to connect my journey to his.

"And that's the chance that you have, whenever you're frustrated. Instead of yelling at the umpire, or even the other players, you can put your focus back into the team and create a vision for winning. Not just when you're hurting. *Especially* when you're hurting. Do you think you can do that?"

"I can," he said, climbing down from the bunk as if he had forgotten all about his challenges with the game that day.

I sat there a moment, allowing myself to exhale for a moment and consider the subtle shift of direction that my vulnerability, and making use of my greatest trials, helped to offer.

Then I rejoined my team at the kitchen table.

Maybe you wish to teach your kids, or guide your employees, or inspire your customers to see the world as you do. No matter the target audience or the need of the particular moment, it's good to cultivate a few *losses and lessons* stories that create connection, reveal wisdom, and show some rough spots you've faced. I would bet that you have had many pivots in your life, many depths plunged, and many insights gathered, that you've not yet developed into stories.

Prompts to help shape your losses into lessons:

- Have you ever failed at something? What did you learn?
- Have you ever had to change an ingrained habit? What happened?
- What was the worst game/project/company situation

you've been a part of? What did you learn?

- Have you ever been fired?
- Share a moment of bad judgment that gave you some good wisdom.

It's a bummer to lose. But once you're on the other side of the valley, looking back with 20/20 hindsight, the losses may give you some of your best stories.

ARRANGE YOUR LOOSE CHANGE

Some of the twists and turns in our lives just don't quite fit in a bucket. How often do you find yourself thinking back to a particularly surprising moment or insight in your life, but don't know where it fits in the big picture? That's loose change. The moments that sit there in your photo album, on your desk, tucked in the couch, or in your memory that you haven't figured out how to apply.

Did you once set out on a journey thinking you had an answer to something, but found out you were very wrong? Did you get some counsel from someone that changed the course of your life? Did someone you despised become your strongest ally? Were you hurt? And how did you heal? Did you find, simply, that "we can't get there from here" and shift course? Questions after questions lead to stories.

Loose change may be misplaced moments that are just out of sight, moments that reappear once in a while without explanation, floating around like asteroids in the constellation of your stories. While it's hard to find stories by simply asking someone to "tell a story," specific invitations can better hone in on specific moments. There are a thousand prompts that can help you find

Victim mentality

your most essential shifts—and help others find theirs, too. What changes seem to survive in your imagination, like a narrative thorn in your side, and make you wonder: why is that memory coming up?

Some ideas to help you gather your loose change:

[handwritten: • LCPD direct mail • Total Plant]

- What was a big project that transformed you?
- Was there a time when you faced a crisis or helped someone through one?
- Have you ever run out of gas—in your car or your body?
- What's one great mountain you've climbed, physically or metaphorically?
- Have you, or has someone close to you, fallen seriously ill, and how did that experience change you?

As you approach one of your stories, give yourself the time to take in the senses. Take in the smells. The sounds. The tension around you. Look for the journeys, coming up with a beginning point and end point. See if they depict a turnaround, an *a-ha* moment, or a deep trial. Was there an *and then one day*? What was the world like before this change? What were *you* like before? After? *[handwritten: so many years of hiding, feeling like failure &]*

Each moment of change can't, of course, become a story. And even if it does, you may not ever share the story. But the practice of finding and shaping this change brings you deeper into your own story-discovery practice. And every story connects to another; the prompts above may lead you to stories that lead you to other prompts.

So practice radical curiosity. Look all around, because every story you hear might prompt another story that has been hiding in the folds of your mind.

[handwritten, right margin: damaged goods.]

THE MIGHT OF INSIGHT

Life is woven with moments of insight where time seems to slow down, and you know that something important is going on. The hard part is capturing these moments, seeing their value in the big picture, and making use of them. At first, the value may be hard to discern.

As James Joyce wrote:

The instant of inspiration is a spark so brief as to be invisible . . . this is the instant in which the word is made flesh.[20]

And the moments we shape can sometimes shape our lives.

One day, Becky Tarbotton, the executive director of Rainforest Action Network, swept into our office. It was my storytelling dream team: my co-founder Joel, who carried 1000 stories in his head; Nell, whose patient support of Becky's story-finding process was unparalleled in a communications director; Becky, who faced every story with vigor and curiosity; and me.

"Something happened last week and I can't stop thinking about it," Becky said. We were working on a keynote, and the topic of the day was how to talk about her organization's recent victory: convincing Disney, the largest publisher in the world, to stop using paper sourced from virgin rainforest.

"I was rushing to catch my plane and finally sat down and ordered a glass of wine, when I recognized this great halo of gray hair," Becky says. Who's sitting in front of her, but David Suzuki, the physicist and climate expert—for whom Becky was an "intern's intern" many years earlier.

"So, we're talking, and after a few minutes, David says, 'Becky, you know, we've lost.'"

Lost?

Becky turned to us. "He was talking about climate change," she said. "We've lost the fight."

Becky's words drifted off. Her anguish was palpable. She had been sitting with this experience for days and days, rolling it over in her head, walking around it, drawing meaning. That was her way with every story she encountered. In fact, Becky had taken to finding stories quite unlike anyone I had met before. Almost immediately after our first meetings, she began using new stories in staff meetings and applying them in her speeches. She was committed, inspired, and was clearly finding her voice.

Certainly, there was the obvious meaning: *we're screwed*. And for a person who had dedicated her life to caring for the earth, hearing this from her mentor sent her reeling. It would put all the work she was doing, all the motivating she did every day—and the meaning of all of it—at risk.

As she finished retelling the scene from the plane, she paused.

"So what did you make of that?" Joel asked. No judgment, no assumptions, just a question. Becky looked up after a long minute. "You know what? Strangely, I felt a sense of relief," she told us. "A sense that we no longer need to fight to stop it." Rather, she decided, *we need to find a way to adapt.* Suddenly the concern washed away from her face.

The insight had become a pivot.

Weeks later, I attended Becky's keynote.[21] In it, she retold the David Suzuki story—one single moment in her busy life—and used it to establish an entirely new perspective on climate change.

After she said that line, "We've lost," you could have heard a pin drop. After all, the audience was made up of people who were utterly committed to reversing climate change. People who would scale a building to unveil this message.

Behind me, a woman gasped. "Nooo . . . ," she said.

"It's true," said Becky. We didn't stop climate change. "But people, look around you. We are not losing." She paused for several seconds.

"This is the year that 124 coal plants have been shuttered. This is the year that Iowa produced 20 percent of its electricity from renewable energy. This is the year that four people talked a $40 billion company into stopping sourcing any paper from the rainforest . . . and that is in no way meant to diminish the urgency of what we're trying to achieve." She said, looking around the room. "It is simply to say that we also need to pay attention to where we're winning."

When Martin Luther King talked about his dream on that August day, he didn't ignore the challenges of the attendees. Rather, he drew them in, and brought them to another place. And that's what Becky did that night, she took the audience along, deep into the innermost cave, and guided them to take on a new journey. Because, she said, "We really are in the midst of what will be the next great industrial revolution...and we're talking about re-embedding the economy within the limits of nature."

Becky felt the moment and, with time, saw how it was an important insight. She found the fruit and recognized it had a seed inside. And with that, she worked to turn the course of an old story into a new one:

We've lost that fight, but pay attention, because a greater challenge is upon us.

You don't have to be a keynote speaker or head of an organization to turn an insight to a story. Your life is woven with them, these key realizations that inform why you do what you do. And they make for good stories—even if not all are clear to the eye. Some you may just have to plant and water. They could be a lesson that someone taught you, or a moment when time seemed to stop, and the world changed before your eyes.

Sometimes our key insights reveal a bold step into the unknown. Sometimes they tap at something dramatic, or even traumatic. They may show how we respond when we're fed up with the way things are—innovation born from frustration. Sometimes our insights are nothing more than a well-framed and surprising teaching that has stayed alive, curiously nagging at us, many years beyond its occurrence, and leaving us with some growth on the other side.

Even everyday statements can take on a different meaning when delivered at the right time, a bit of wisdom brought by a mentor who can see the value of the moment. This insight may be just the thing to create your *until finally* moment.

Maybe your insights just hang there, suspended in memory, and seem strange to retell. Maybe they are sparked by reading a book, or watching a movie, or mourning a loved one. Or maybe they're more obscure, and need some searching and discovery.

So take a deeper look across time and consider the might of your insights, and why they might matter to you now.

Some prompts that might help you find them:

- Who has helped you understand leadership, just at the right moment?
- Have you ever had a near-death experience? What did you learn?
- What obstacles have you overcome professionally?
- What is one innovation your organization has achieved? Was there a moment that turned the dial?
- What was your best idea? What happened with it?

Not everything, of course, is fodder for stories. Our key insights aren't always retellable. Sometimes we let the fruit fall, uncertain of how—or if—to share them. Sometimes the change is not apparent. Sometimes, quite simply, we're too *in the story*, too deep in the innermost cave, not quite ready to emerge, and it's not ready to tell. But sometimes we haven't looked up long enough to know that the lessons have actually been learned, and it's time to share them. Sometimes an insight is just needing an *ever since then* to become a story.

As your practice strengthens, you'll begin to see lessons more often. You will hear a story and consider "why was it so good?" or "why was it so bad?" And these reflections will inform the stories that build your constellation.

SUGGESTION: A STORY BOX

How often do you lose things, like your phone? Your keys? You wander to and fro, looking places you've already looked (under the seat) and random places (in the trunk), and when you try to pull up the memory of exactly what you did, you come up blank.

Things get lost easily in this busy world, both the smallest things and the largest things. Even the most precious things go astray for a moment—like your most valuable insights, the great lessons you've learned, and some of your most poignant stories.

Do you ever find yourself preparing for a speech, or a blog, or a meeting with a customer, knowing you want to open with just the right story, but when you think about it, you just get white noise?

Here is my tip for the day to help you keep hold of your stories: Get a story box. With a story box, you will remember your most prized insights and lessons and will be more likely to call them up when you most need them.

This is how to do it:

1. **Get a box.** Make it something nicely designed . . . an old cigar box or jewelry box. Mine is a wooden box from Marrakesh that the great storyteller Joel ben Izzy (who

also happens to be my cofounder) gifted me.

2. **Break them down into different levels of readiness.** Include three different types of stories, which can also be three colors of notecards: *go-tos*, *reserves*, and *key insights*.

3. **Spend ten minutes thinking of the stories you already tell—your *go-tos*.** These might be in presentations, keynotes, or even at dinner parties. Write them on different cards. Then write down the *reserves* and *key insights*.

4. **Keep it simple!** A few lines, maybe a title for the story, an opening line, and a few talking points that will help you remember. Consider outlining your key pivots: *And then one day*, *until finally*, and *ever since then*. If you have it, include the last line of the story—the landing point. Don't try stuffing presentation scripts or five-page written stories in there. This is about stories you can tell in a variety of different ways to a variety of different audiences.

5. **Develop them.** In the days that follow, keep thinking about stories you tell. They'll likely appear over time. If you're at your desk, great; if not, put them in your wallet or in your phone to save for when you get to your story box.

6. **If you don't have complete stories, don't worry about it!** Look for ideas, seeds of stories. Once you give them a little attention and some sunlight, they'll grow quickly.

7. **Tell them.** The best way to remember your stories, of course, is to practice them. So look at your stories every few days, and tell them to friends, in meetings, or in presentations. Push your edge. And when you're looking for stories, review your other cards, too. This will help strengthen your entire story collection.

You may prefer to keep your stories in a Word doc on your desktop, or in a list of notes on your phone. Regardless, the more you care for your stories, the more you'll develop them, the more you'll remember them . . . and the more you'll use them.

Your stories are not carved into stone tablets. They are living, breathing signposts, and always ready to be reshaped. How you gather your ideas, how you speak of your work in the world, how you speak of your accomplishments, and how you face your failures, each may change. For every story you have ever told may move and shift on any given day, infusing each lesson with new perspective, and each retelling with new vigor.

Chapter 6

THE STORY-SHAPING PROCESS

One with the Audience. Anchor the Moments.
Zoom In, Zoom Out. Spark Suspense. Use Funny.
Get Thyself a Story Buddy. When You Get to the End.

ONE WITH THE AUDIENCE

When Ken Dychtwald, longtime entrepreneur, noted futurist, author of sixteen books, and keynote speaker with 40 years of experience, tells a story, I listen. In a story session one day, Ken told me about an experience from his early twenties, when he worked at the Esalen Institute in Big Sur, California. Ken had heard that the great Indian sitar player Ravi Shankar, teacher of the Beatles, was coming to the Bay Area. So he and some fellow friends piled in a VW bus and headed north.

A few hours later, the friends arrived in a hall on the University of California campus. "I'm sitting in lotus position," Ken said. "Then Ravi Shankar comes in. He's tuning his sitar for quite a while. Five minutes later he's still tuning his sitar. We're waiting and waiting, and he tunes for ten minutes, and he tunes for fifteen minutes." He tuned for thirty minutes, and then, as Ken said, "He starts to really play." The show was amazing.

A few weeks later, Shankar happened to come to Esalen,

where he played another mind-blowing show. Afterward, Ken went up to him. "Mr. Shankar, I went to your show in Berkeley a few weeks ago, and you were tuning your sitar for so long. Can you just tell me—what was the problem?"

Shankar looked up at him, head swaying slightly side to side.

"Ken. I was not tuning my sitar."

"Excuse me?" asked Ken, wondering what he was missing.

"I was tuning the audience."

And so it is for you, storyteller. Every step of your story is a tuning:

- How do you set up the story?
- How much do you anchor in detail?
- How do you zoom across time?
- How do you draw them in, and how do you provide the payoff?

Think of your audience. Who are they? What is the change you want to bring them through? Where are they now—in terms of their knowledge and their beliefs—and where do you want them to be? What might be their hurdles in getting there?

A retellable story is not about charisma, or eye contact, or a good script. It's about tuning your audience—that is, knowing the journey you're creating well enough so you can take them along, anchoring in the key moments, adeptly revealing the twists and turns, and landing your message when you arrive at the end.

ANCHOR THE MOMENTS

"I sent you a table with a red cloth on it, a cage, a rabbit, and the number eight in blue ink. You saw them all, especially that blue eight. We've engaged in an act of telepathy."

—Stephen King, *On Writing*

Details matter. As the storyteller, you are the guide, taking your audience with you out of the room. But you can't simply talk about the key pivots in your story. You have to anchor your story into place, and in the emotions of the moment, so your audience will feel connected to the experience. It's part of the magic of story.

So as you shape yours, some questions to consider:

- Who are you talking about?
- What do they look like?
- Where are they? What's the weather like; is anything distinct about the room?
- What details can you share about how the characters look, or how they move?
- If it's you, how were you different then? Were you younger? Did you wear funny shoes?

The sensory details of the key moments enhance the feeling of the experience you unfold. We can go there with you, to the soft floor of a forest of redwoods, or a rooftop's edge atop an eighty-story building, or to the strange texture of escargot at a fancy French restaurant. We feel the cool grass, the tension of the boardroom, and the draft coming in through the cracked window of your first office.

Stacking senses helps. In his book *Moonwalking with Einstein*, Joshua Foer follows around a memory champion—one of those guys who can memorize a thousand digits in a row or the Declaration of Independence backwards—in order to learn how to remember things better. As the memory expert says:

"The more associative hooks a new piece of information

has, the more securely it gets embedded into the network of things you already know, and the more likely it is to remain in memory."[22]

Remain in memory. A-ha! The more the sensory details—sound, sight, taste, smell, touch—the more real the story becomes in your listener's mind, and the more likely he is to remember the story. If you include a description of an alley, that's one thing. But if you talk about a dark alley filled with the squeaky utterings of mice, or a racing cat carrying a stinky day-old fish, your description is much more likely to remain in memory.

If you talk about a man on a raft, that's one thing. But when he's sitting in the blazing sun, with no food for days, and the sharks start circling . . . you get the picture.

According to Dr. Paul Zak, the neuroscientist who studies stories:

"Scientists liken attention to a spotlight. We are only able to shine it on a narrow area. If that area seems less interesting than some other area, our attention wanders."

Attention, especially these days, is scarce. How long do you go without your attention wandering back to your phone? Even in a world not flooded with new information, it takes a lot of brain resources to focus. Using the *attention spotlight* is an investment that your brain makes; focusing on only one thing at a time can be dangerous, so there's got to be a good reason to do so. Give your audience a good reason!

Zak continues: "Once a story has sustained our attention long enough, we may begin to emotionally resonate with story's characters. Narratologists call this 'transportation.'"[23]

The ability to direct and refresh the attention spotlight is to be a good guide, drawing your audience members into an experience and drawing them out of it in a way that feels rewarding.

Each key pivot in the Journey Curve can be anchored in a

moment. When you set the scene, we begin to see the world of your creation; we feel what the characters feel, and the change becomes real. When you don't anchor in the moments, we contemplate what time we'll eat dinner or think about that show we saw last night.

Pivoting around a particular object can help: an old watch, a tree swing, or an antique spoon, for example. My dad used to tell a story about his job as a timer for the University of Oregon track team in the late 1950s. One day, he says, the track coach came to practice shaking his head. "My wife is going to kill me," said the coach, holding a pair of track shoes with rubber bumps melted into the sole. "I ruined another waffle iron."

The coach, named Bill Bowerman, years later would go on to cofound a small shoe company by the name of Nike. Today, there is a statue at the University of Oregon of Bowerman standing on a waffle iron. And Bowerman's artifacts are so important to the Nike story that the recent discovery of some old waffle irons in his backyard went directly to the Nike museum.

ZOOM IN, ZOOM OUT

Daedalus, the great inventor in ancient Greece, had gone too far. He crossed his employer King Minos, the ruler of Crete, and for this was imprisoned with his son Icarus in a tower high above the sea.

For days on end, Daedalus stared out at the sea, refusing to give up. But the port was constantly guarded. The land was patrolled.

Then one day, as he observed the seagulls flying by, he realized that if he could gather their feathers and fasten them together with candle wax, he could build wings, and together he and Icarus could escape. The skies, he saw, were the only way out.

So, they gathered, glued, and tested. And eventually, they stood on the edge of the cliff, with their giant wings ready to fly. Daedalus looked down at his son and said:

"Now Icarus, don't fly too high or too low. If you soar too high, the sun will melt the wax, and you'll fall to your death. If you fly too low, the salt water will soak your wings, and you'll drown."

The story doesn't end well. Icarus, it turns out, loves the heights. Daedalus warns him to stay the middle road, but compelled to fly higher and higher, Icarus soars up close to the sun. Finally, the wax begins to melt, and the feathers begin to fall . . . and Icarus plummets to his death.

A foreboding tale, to be sure.

But in the context of the retellable story, I want to bring you a similar message. *Don't fly too high or too low.*

You need to reach the heights, to zoom out to give the big picture. But if you fly too high and tell your story with too little detail, your audience won't *feel* the challenge you're facing. Yet the opposite, staying too low, zooming in too closely to the ground without coming back up, leaving us all soaked in too many details, is the other side of the coin.

A good story relies largely on how adeptly you zoom in and zoom out across time. So strike the right balance, soaring high for perspective, and going lower so we can see the ground.

Zoom out too far for too long, and you can risk losing the wings of your story. How often have you heard a story where someone just flies too high?

When we first launched our company, things were okay. And as we became more successful, I found a way to deal with adversity. Now we're doing great!

Can you see anything in the mind's eye? Can you see a clear vision of what was happening? A bunch of people working in an attic? Half-filled coffee cups? Are they up all night? Crying to their girlfriends or boyfriends? Sending away creditors at the door? Do you feel something in your body when the story is told?

Without dropping down into the scene and showing the adversity you faced, we may not go with you.

The opposite of flying too high is flying too low, zooming in too closely to the ground without coming back. What if I told you this:

We opened our doors on December 12, 2000, and at first, things were okay. The first two years were pretty steady. The year 2002 was a little difficult, and we nearly had to close. Especially in the fall, right before our relaunch—that was a really hard time. We had many phone calls with investors and many difficult meetings. I remember one lunch in particular where we didn't even have a chance to eat before we were turned down. Oh, yes, and the many late nights . . .

At about the third line, you can tell I may not be going anywhere. And suddenly, impatience comes to the forefront! The story is at risk of plummeting into the sea.

So don't tell it all. No one has thirty-five years to hear your thirty-five-year-long journey. With too many details and too little motion, we begin to lose trust in our teller. When distrust creeps in and we don't know what the point of the story is, and its relevance to our current challenges, our thoughts begin to drift back to our schedules, our emails, that strange-looking painting on the wall . . .

This is where your Journey Curve can help. How was the world before? What emblematic moment can you test out? What was your *and then one day*? Zoom in to help us connect with the scene, and then move through it to the next one.

Zooming in and zooming out helps you keep momentum and direction in your story, while drawing us in to the emotions and the details. It keeps the balance between soaring and soaking.

SPARK SUSPENSE

When you were in high school, did you learn the following writing mantra?

"Tell them what you're going to say, say it, then tell them what you said."

That's what I learned. And although it got me through many papers and presentations, what I've found is that when it comes to telling a story, this is the worst advice. Telling the ending at the beginning is one of the best ways to ruin a story.

Today I'm going to show you that . . . Stop! Don't do it! Don't tell them what you're going to say. Keep them guessing.

"But people are busy!" you say. "I have to get to the point!"

But here's my question: Do you have to *get to the point*, or do you have to make sure *they get the point*?

So, yes, it can be valuable to allude to what will happen. To foreshadow the problem, give your audience clues along the road.

Things were all set up perfectly . . . or so we thought.

And then the phone rang.

But then something unexpected happened.

Each of these clues takes the audience around the corner, building just a little tension to set up for a payoff.

So don't telegraph your story. Nothing is less satisfying than the movie trailer that tells everything. When you're speaking, use pauses. Make use of suspense, and hold the next moment of your story. Take your time. Tune your audience. Sense where they are in the story. Get them curious, and ready them for a change.

Whether it's a one-minute story or a ten-minute story, you always have the opportunity to draw them a little deeper into the journey.

Get us saying "And then what happened?" And we'll be in the world of your creation, feeling what you feel, remembering what you remember.

USE FUNNY

Comedy is a great tool for enhancing your storytelling, creating connection, and getting your audience to relax, opening them more deeply to your message—and having more fun.

I'm not talking about using jokes. I don't recommend jokes! I mean using irony and contrast, honing in on surprising and unique moments that can create more connection. An entire book could be written on this topic—and has.

I talked recently with someone who wrote such a book: David Nihill, stand-up comic and founder of the presentation company FunnyBiz. Terrified of public speaking growing up, David would stand up in front of class and struggle to keep his paper from shaking. It was so bad, in fact, that his classmates began calling him "Shaking Stevens." He decided face his fear by dedicating two years to following comics and performing on various comedy stages. The results of his journey can be found in his book *Do You Talk Funny? 7 Comedy Habits to Become a Better (and Funnier) Public Speaker.*

"I don't know if you can make *any* story funny, but I believe that everyone's funny," David told me. "You're never going to be funny for all people all the time. But if it makes you laugh, it will probably make others laugh."

David writes about his opening line at one of San Francisco's biggest comedy clubs: "I am from Ireland so I do have a bit of an accent. If I say something funny and you guys don't laugh, I'm going to assume you didn't understand, and just say it again."

The line got the audience laughing. So he tried it again the next time on stage. Now it's one of his *go-to* lines, and it never seems to get old.

Here are some steps he shared to lift up your funny game. Luckily, each one reinforces your story practice:

1. **Play with sequence.** Sometimes just by changing the order of how you tell the story, you find something funny.

2. **Don't put yourself up so high.** If you're the CEO, you need to have some form of self-deprecation to bring you down to the level of everyone else. As David says, "To laugh with you, they have to like you."

3. **Build suspense.** Don't tell it all at the beginning. And don't say the joke line first. Build to it.

4. **Get into the details.** Look closely. If it's not funny, go deeper into the specifics to find the funny things about it, something relatable and quirky. Ask a dozen questions: What was he wearing? Where did she go afterwards? What did they do?

5. **Compare and contrast.** Explore how you're thinking or what you're concluding, and identify the opposite. This can free up your thinking process.

6. **Record it and replicate.** You may know you're going to get a laugh; you just don't know when or know how big. When you record your talk and listen to it, you'll find out which parts work and which parts you need to rework.

7. **Get on stage.** The more you're on stage, the better. So warm up with an open mic or go to a Toastmasters group. A storytelling night. Anything that puts you in front of a group of people will make you more comfortable. Tell stories at dinner and work on the funny pieces. When you're on stage, you'll feel what's working. Remember these elements and try them again next time.

8. **Rinse and repeat!**

GET THYSELF A STORY BUDDY

Storytelling is a practice. And the most important thing to do sometimes is find someone with whom to practice!

Stories happen everywhere—shiny little gems of meaning lining the path of your day—whether in a conference room or a café.

As your skills develop, you'll have more opportunities to share your stories and help others find and tell their own. You may find, in fact, that your story ears are becoming attuned—as you listen to stories on TV, in podcasts, in meetings, at dinner, or on the subway.

In order to dive deeper into the stories you're finding each day, and to help build out your repertoire, get a story buddy. Call a friend, or a coworker who may also be interested in working on her stories. Share stories over coffee once a week. They might be as simple as something you heard yesterday or a story from your *reserves* that you've been shaping.

Here are some steps to follow to be a better story buddy:

1. Become a story listener.

First and foremost, give the story your full attention. Put to the side your judgment and any ideas of where the story should go.

Whether your story buddy is solely listening to you or you are helping each other, it's worthwhile to remember how difficult it can be to tell any story the first time. So as you begin, hold the bar for success very low. Agree with your partner that the first goal is practice.

So listen fully. Be compassionate. Be generous. Don't interrupt! Sometimes, just giving your attention is the most wonderful offering.

Listen between the lines for what is *not* being said. Maybe your buddy gets stuck in the problem, or he tells a story that soars too high and doesn't quite bring you down to the ground. Maybe he doesn't give proper context to set up a satisfying change, and maybe there's no change at all. As you listen, ask yourself, *what is this story really about*?

2. Get curious.

Ask yourself some questions to help hone the story:

- How did the story begin?
- Did you feel transported, immersed, surprised?
- Did the story take you to the ground, then zoom across time?
- Were there clear pivots? Either explicit or implicit *one day*, or *until finally*, or *ever since then*?
- Would more context be valuable? Or less?
- What was the key takeaway for you?
- What changed as a result? Did your perspective change?
- Would you recommend more contrast?
- Could you retell the story?

As you go through the story, consider the Journey Curve, and how this story could become more retellable. Pay attention to the change your buddy depicts and any lesson he may have learned. Ask clarifying questions.

3. Share the things you like.

First share the positive, and then reveal what you feel is needed to improve the story. This might sound obvious, but it's not. It's hard sometimes, when you feel like a story isn't working. But put that aside, and think about what works. It will open up a clearer opportunity for learning between the two of you.

Then work with your buddy to tell the story again. If, tomorrow, you find you are compelled to retell the story, let your buddy know!

WHEN YOU GET TO THE END

Stop!

It's always good to know just where you're going and how you're going to land your journey. So know your last line. And do your best to stick to it. You'll be happy you did.

There are a thousand directions that your story may travel. But once it is released, you can never know its full potential, because your story travels outwards at the speed of life.

Chapter 7

SHARE THEM

Matching the Message to the Story. Two Thousand
Times a Charm. Getting to the Core. The Pitch is Dead,
Long Live the Pitch! Enlisting Your Wider Circle.
Troubleshoot, Again and Again.

There once was a great storyteller that lived in the region that we now call Ukraine. His name was Dubno Maggid; the teacher of the city of Dubno.

Dubno Maggid would tell a story at a wedding, and everyone would cry. He'd tell a story to two fighting kids, and they'd quickly become friends. He'd tell a story to a captured thief, and the thief would mend his ways.

One day, his friend, Rabbi Elijah, asked him a question. "Dubno Maggid, how is it that you always have the right story for every occasion?" The Dubno Maggid looked at him and said, "Let me tell you a story."

There was once a prince who was a very good archer. But he wanted to be a great archer. So he traveled across the land to learn from a master, and after many years returned, having accomplished his goal. On his way back, he stopped at a farm to get some food. And there, he saw the most amazing thing. There, on the side of a barn, the prince saw ten targets, each with an arrow right in the bulls-eye. The prince was dumbfounded. He asked the farmer, 'Did you do this?'

'Me? No. That was my son Yekle.' Over walks Yekle. He's about eleven years old, dragging a bow behind him. 'Yekle!' said the prince. 'How did you do this?!'

Yekle looked up at him. 'First, I had to lift the bow up, like this,' he said as he raised the bow and pulled an arrow from his quiver. 'Then, I place the arrow like so . . . and zing!' he said, hitting the side of the barn. 'Then, I get out some black paint, and ever so carefully, I draw a great big circle around the arrow. And then I take the white paint . . .'

"And so," says the Dubno Maggid. "It's not about the right story for every occasion, but instead finding the right occasion for a story."

And so it is for you, too, good reader. As you gather your stories, and as you practice them, you'll find more and more opportunities to share them in different ways with different audiences. The focus is not on the bulls-eye, but to be *in the practice*.

So gather your stories, and have them ready in your quiver. Then, when the right moment arises, deliver the story, and draw a circle around it, shaping the meaning to meet the need of the moment.

MATCHING THE MESSAGE TO THE STORY

As you tell your story, a few people in the audience might have a question that they're not asking.

The question is this: "Why are you telling me this?"

Maybe they're just excited to get the upshot. Or maybe they're impatient, or even skeptical you're taking them somewhere worth going.

Don't worry. It's natural. Because as long as you know where you're going, and you're controlling the vehicle, all is well. You are building to your message, the purpose you have for telling the story.

But here's the catch: your message needs to be a good one. And everything in your story has to lead to it.

By good, I mean relevant. Relevant to the moment and to the audience.

The message of your story is not a data point, and doesn't have to be a "moral." And there can't be five. Just one. The message of your story is the treasure your story carries, the one you wish to unveil to this particular audience at this particular time.

Tune the audience.

When things are hard, put your focus back into the team.

Don't let your communications get stuck in the hair.

Each of your stories may deliver a slightly a different message depending on the moment. And there are different ways of finding that message, depending on your starting point. Here are three:

1. You've got a story, but lack the right message.

Sometimes I find that a story has a way of calling out. *I want to be told*, it says. *I've got something to say!* You may not know why at first, but with some consideration, it becomes clearer. Sometimes, when I'm puzzling about the purpose of a story, I go back to the moment in question, get as specific to the moment as I can, and freeze the scene.

Once you have thought of the story you want to tell, or when you're practicing telling the story in a different way than you've told it before, you can ask yourself: *Why do I want to tell this?*

As you prepare, scan across the story, and ask: *What is this story really about?* Depending on the timing and the audience, it could be about a few different things. Look around at the sequence of events. Are you getting it? What is happening here? Do you need to drop a scene or two? Or add one?

Keep asking until you are sure . . . sure enough to tell it, at least—it may well change later.

2. You're looking for the right story for your message.

You know the message you want to share and are looking for the right story to land that message.

Most likely, there are a few messages that you deliver already. Things you find yourself saying over and over again in a variety of different ways.

Each of these key messages would be well suited to have matching stories. Largely, this comes back to the work of developing your repertoire, mixing and matching. What stories do you tell already? What stories are in your *reserves* that you've not quite yet told, but that could be developed now?

This process of matching stories to messages doesn't all happen in real time, of course, five minutes before you give a talk, or when you're having a difficult conversation with a team member. But as you develop your collection of stories, and are more readily able to draw from it, these moments will occur more and more. A need will arise, a message will emerge, and a story will appear. Then it's just a matter of tuning the story to land your message.

When you are able to match that message to a story, it becomes a gift. It's a gift because it carries an insight—distinct information about how the world works, applied with intention and care. It's a gift because you've considered your audience deeply.

And because you've delivered it at just the right time.

3. You have no message yet, but you do have a moment.

So, there are the times when you have a story and times when you have a message. At yet other times you simply have a particular audience and a particular moment. Maybe no stories are emerging, and no message seems completely clear.

In these times, consider these questions as you consider your audience:

Where am I right now? Where are they right now?

That is: *what do I need? What do they need?*

And as you consider this, ask: *What do I want to say to them right now to meet them where they are?*

Sometimes the destination of the story—the message, the lesson, the key data point—is worth developing first. Find the place you want to take your audiences, and then go looking for a story that will take them there.

TWO THOUSAND TIMES A CHARM

In the fall of 1974, Ken Dychtwald was wrapping up his first book, *BodyMind*, about harnessing the innate intelligence of the body. Knowing his work, a friend invited him to lead a body/mind therapy group for men and women in their seventies and eighties.

While initially resistant to the work—keep in mind the going philosophy was "Don't trust anyone over thirty"—Ken had agreed to a short-term project. "But soon, I was hooked," says Ken. "I became absolutely fascinated with older people. I realized that if you could see past the way they dressed, the wrinkles and gray hair, these were often towering figures, seasoned men and women who had a vast perspective on life." Suddenly, Ken saw things through the lens of older people, and saw how utterly unprepared American society was for the coming aging population: how difficult newspapers were to read, how difficult door handles were for arthritic hands to open, and how hard stairs were to climb for weakening legs.

Fast forward a few years, and Ken was speaking around the country on issues of the aging population. One day, he was having lunch with his friend and mentor Maggie Kuhn, founder of the Gray Panthers, a group that advocated for the rights of elders. Maggie was then in her late seventies, and in her talks, she often would raise her wrinkled arm and say, "Revolution until rigor mortis!"

She looked over at Ken and said, "Ken, do you like the story that you're telling?"

Ken said, "I do. I like this story very much."

And Maggie said, "Well that's great, because you'll need to tell it two thousand more times."

"Two thousand more times?" Ken said. "I have no idea how many times is two thousand when it comes to telling a story!"

But he kept telling it, this story about the coming of aging boomers, the demographics and needs of this population, and how we must change things to prepare for their arrival. Over and over again he told the story to senators, to CEOs, and to students. He cofounded a company called AgeWave and enlisted the leaders of countries, leaders of cities, and leaders of the healthcare industry. He told the story in one hundred different ways, through media appearances, through anecdotes, in product meetings, in books, and in every conversation, for many years. New products, new laws, new organizations grew out of this story, when others began to see what he saw.

Eventually, he did tell it two thousand times—and he kept going. And by some accounts, Ken has told his story in person to over two million people, and has been seen by nearly 30,000,000 people on television.

When it comes to your own story, if you are working every day to address a problem that needs solving, either on your own or with your company, be prepared to tell it two thousand times. Short version, long version, tweeted version, or blogged version. Each time you tell your story—through supporting stories, data points out in the world that reinforce your story, allies that are contributing to it, and examples that show that things are changing—the people around you become a part of it. And with each retelling, the story comes more and more to life.

GETTING TO THE CORE

As you get more in contact with the many stories you are telling, you'll see a greater story begin to form. This story convergence may be called for in everyday ways such as in job interviews, on your bio, or in partnership conversations. It also may appear in big ways, informing your keynote, your company story, or your writings. But it appears, much like Ken's story, every day.

This bigger story is your core story. Your core story depicts your greater journey and reveals the "why" of what you do—why you are the person for a certain job, why you set out on a certain endeavor, and, most importantly, why you care.

Meaning: It's not just a story about serving your customers. It's about you, what's most important to you, what sets you apart—and what will keep you going when things are hard.

Like an accordion, a core story expands and contracts, and it can be shared in many different ways, drawing in various insights for different purposes and audiences. It doesn't have to be long—it might be as short as one minute or as long as five.

And to share a core story means to be able to tell several of your stories—such as your origin, your impact, and your vision—and put them together in different ways.

Five years ago, my cofounder Joel and I were in Columbia, Maryland, working on a core story project for a new client, Enterprise Community Partners. As we walked around the office and the grounds outside, I noted many interesting pictures of their deceased founder, Jim Rouse. I saw his face on the cover of *Time Magazine*, a statue outside next to the lake, and photographs with American presidents. Jim was one of the most successful developers of his era: he built neighborhoods, some of the early shopping centers, and an entire city, Columbia, where Enterprise is headquartered. Instead of retiring and heading to the golf course, Jim founded Enterprise at the age of sixty-eight. He spent his later years working every day—and mostly every night—to create healthy and affordable housing for the communities that were hardest to serve, those at the bottom rung of the financial ladder.

I was especially intrigued by the company's bold vision:

One day, every person will have an affordable home in a vibrant community, filled with promise and the opportunity for a good life.

Wow. That's a big vision, I thought to myself. In fact, the more I learned, the more my *why-o-meter* went off. That's the most important question in creating any story: Why? Why does this matter to you? Why now? Why you?

And that's just what I was asking myself: *Why did Jim Rouse take on this great journey?* Why, when most people were retiring, would a man of his success create an organization to unveil such a massive vision? "Because it's important" is not a good answer. What made this guy tick?

In my conversations and readings, I found out something

about his origins: when Jim was sixteen, at the beginning of the Depression, his father's business failed. His mother then fell ill, and so did his father. Both died within a year—and then the banks foreclosed on the family home.

Jim Rouse, the founder of a national organization that has helped thousands of people find homes, was a homeless orphan.

Okay, so that gave us a real sense of why he might do this. Jim knew what it felt like. It also made sense that he had spent a large part of his career building communities: because he knew what it felt like to lose one.

Then we needed *the how*. That is, what's the special sauce that has made all of this magic happen—and is still making it happen, years after his death, in a five-hundred-person organization? And how can that be brought to life?

It came in the story of three women.

Then one day in the spring of 1973, three women from Jim's church approached him with an idea. Where they lived, in the Adams Morgan neighborhood of Washington, DC, were two of the worst tenements they had ever seen. Seeing the lack of decent housing for people with very limited means, they asked a simple question: Why not buy the buildings and fix them up, so people can live in decent housing with dignity?

His career as a developer gave Jim a hundred reasons why the idea wouldn't work. He thought it was crazy and said as much. Thinking that was the end of it, he was shocked when the three women soon returned. "We did it!" they said. "Did what?" Jim asked. "We made a down payment on those buildings!" He was stunned by their audacity. But more than that, he was amazed at their commitment. Calling their group Jubilee, they had raised funds from everyone in the church and put down a nonrefundable deposit. They were absolutely determined to succeed.

Jim knew well what it takes to get deals done—technical expertise, financing know-how, the right connections, the ability to negotiate government channels, and a lot of hard work. What these women had, though, was a critical link—a dedication to their own neighborhood and a real understanding of its needs. So he joined them as a partner, working alongside the residents to correct hundreds of housing violations, cleaning up from years of disrepair and poor management. All together, it took 60,000 hours of work, but they renovated those buildings. It was the start of a transformation for the Adams Morgan neighborhood—and the birth of a true social enterprise.[24]

Jim understood financing, he understood working between the public and private sector, and he understood providing needed services to communities. What he had been missing—and what became a key part of the Enterprise platform—these three women provided: real commitment on the ground, in the neighborhood about which they truly cared.

Fast-forward thirty years, and Enterprise invests several billion dollars each year in carrying out its mission. Every day someone moves into a better place to live because of their work.

Today, the core story informs the Enterprise narrative—across videos, speeches, brochures, blogs, and testimony on Capitol Hill. For example, here's how the story showed up on the cover of the annual report:

> From the dreams of a young man
> Who had lost his home,
> Forged with a lifetime of experience,
> Arose a vision for the original social enterprise,
> Bringing together the people and pieces
> We need to transform today's challenges
> Into tomorrow's opportunities.

And home is where it all begins.

Their core story is informed by a clear origin, supported by visible impacts, and given lift by that truly inspiring, connected vision:

One day, every person will have an affordable home in a vibrant community, filled with promise and the opportunity for a good life.[24]

Your core story shows how you got here today. It expands and contracts depending on the audience and the need. It may mean drawing out three key twists in your journey that land your vision. Perhaps it will be an extended version of your origin story, simply ending with your vision: *And that's why, today, we work toward . . .* Or maybe you'll emphasize an impact story, framed with a little more information about your beginnings. But the approach is the same: shape your stories, anchor in key moments, and find how they fit together.

It's a story that you may end up telling two thousand times, so find a way to make it rewarding—not just for the listener, but for the teller.

THE PITCH IS DEAD, LONG LIVE THE PITCH!

But hold on now. What about when you don't have five minutes for your core story, or even two minutes. What about when you have only thirty seconds?

"So your story is like your elevator pitch?" This is a question I'm often asked.

And the answer, in short, is no.

Why? Well, quite simply, because the elevator pitch is dead. The mythology of the elevator pitch harkens back to a time in

Hollywood where screenwriters would need to convince producers of their idea in thirty seconds. Their one chance to push the idea into the producer's head.

Your story isn't about forcing information. We already know everyone around us is information saturated. Your story is about what will survive until tomorrow. It's about a reality that you're creating.

An elevator pitch, when standing alone, can sound robotic: "I work for the leading company in the . . ." or seem defined by tax status: "I work for a 501c3 that . . ." or feel like an out-of-context question: "Have you ever wondered why . . . ?"

I can hear the chains pulling up the drawbridge and the castle doors closing.

You don't need to pitch. You need to *connect*. Connect with something that feels authentic rather than memorized. And of course, you do need to make a quick impression. That's why your story is like an accordion. Once you know how to tell it, you can shorten it and cater it to the needs of the moment, and the needs of the audience.

You do need to be memorable. But your short version is not intended to sell on its own. It's intended to incite curiosity, to draw questions from your audience, whether at a cocktail party, on a plane ride, or during a presentation.

So let's come back to the Journey Curve. What is the essential change of your story? Or, if there are a few, what's the most retellable? How was the world before, and how is it now? Where is the *until finally* moment?

A short retell is a small adventure—a gift rather than an intrusion—even in an elevator or at a cocktail party. Try telling the story more quickly: the world was like this, then something happened, and now everything is different . . . and *ever since then . . .*

Our founder was on a big bike ride, and incredibly hungry, but he couldn't eat one more of those rubbery bars. So he holed up in his mom's kitchen, setting out to make a better bar, until finally, Clif Bar was created.

The story is not a result—it's a journey. Don't fall back into the land of explanation just because you feel you're out of time. Go back in time. Begin in the past and move into discovery. Depending on your audience, you might share more depth about the trial your organization faces, or the results you've achieved.

As you prep for the elevator:

- **Share where you most care.** Your story can reveal a key insight that is relevant to your audience without having to explain what you do or what your company does. Instead of saying "what you do," tell them instead something that reminds you *why you do what you do.*

- **Explore your path to discovery.** Just like in the longer version, the destination is important. That's where you'll really hold the story—and the audience—in your hands. And as you cultivate curiosity, the conversation will optimally lead to questions, and that will be where the real connection happens. So be ready at any time to share more. Perhaps you'll be asked to go more into your origin, your impact, or your vision of change—so this is a chance to pull from your repertoire.

- **Avoid terms that separate.** Instead of "we are" or "the company," use "I help" or "I look for" or "I work to."

- **Get current.** Consider what you did today. Consider an emblematic moment you had last week that represents your greater journey. "Well, last month, I . . ." Your title and company name are only so relevant, even if they're known—and being known may result only in various projections about what people think they know about you.

We all get swept up in the challenges we're facing, and in the pressures of time. So take a moment to tell a story of something about which you care deeply. Think of the good parts, the things that inspire you, and talk about those. While your memorized mission statement might be off-putting, your passion is contagious, and a key variable in a retellable story.

ENLISTING YOUR WIDER CIRCLE

As your stories become more retellable, and as you continue to tell them, you will inevitably gain more allies in your story. But there is also the situation when you need certain people—like your team members or board members or immediate network—to be advocates, whether or not they are compelled to retell your story right away. In this case they may need an extra nudge.

I received an unusually early call on this topic recently from my friend Arpad.

"Question for you," he said, as I brewed my tea. "How can my staff learn which stories to tell to which people—and when?"

Arpad's family has a wine company called Tricycle. They were just opening a new tasting room, and had an urgent need to draw team members into their company story—or, rather, the many stories that were mostly held in the minds of the founding team.

In our previous discussions, we had explored many of them: His dad left Hungary in 1956 and later bought a small Napa vineyard; his brother went back to Hungary and imported barrels; Arpad and his brother took over the vineyards by the Bay and added one in the mountains. Many stories.

"They can't tell all of the stories," Arpad said, "And it seems unnatural to put all of them together while pouring a glass of pinot."

But the question remained, and it was timely: how could he

help the employees know which stories to tell which customers?

Here are my thoughts for when you find yourself in a similar situation, with the need to enlist your team to tell your stories.

1. Look at each of your stories as journeys that depict change.

You likely have many stories, and each one has a "before" and an "after." Each story carries some tension, and some suspense, and some payoff—it in some way reveals how the world was, and what happened to bring the change you're creating.

Give your team the key pivots that they can hold in their hands. Anchor them in time and space. Explore with them the "before" and the "after" of each of your stories, and share why this is important. Did you learn something, create something, or discover something? The more your team perceives the changes along the way that built your company, your values, and your products, the more comfortable they'll feel with the stories.

2. Invite curiosity about the audience.

Invite your team members to be curious: What is the audience's journey, and what are the audience members' needs? Where are they from, why they are visiting, and what do they like? The point is not to teach market research. The point is to reinforce human connection by capturing actionable insights.

3. Connect the dots between audience and story.

The more your team members know your stories, and the more they understand your customer's needs on a very organic level, the better they can link the stories to the customer. In Tricycle's case, out-of-towners may appreciate the contrast between the grapes by the Bay and those from higher elevations. An older couple might be interested in the journey of a man who left Hungary during the revolution and brought with him a passion for grapes. Younger audiences might appreciate more the story of a young adventurer returning to his family's homeland to start a barrel-importing company, or the expertise of bringing the wine, the barrels, and the grapes together into one label.

Apply the pivots based on what you discover. Some customers will ask questions, and others will want to quietly enjoy the tasting.

You'll know soon enough.

TROUBLESHOOT, AGAIN AND AGAIN

Stories reflect life, and as in life, there are many pitfalls in storytelling. Sometimes the story never leaves the ground. Sometimes it doesn't land; it just circles and circles in the sky. Lots of information, wrapped in a long explanation, but the pieces don't come together. You wait for the payoff, and wait, and wait. Or, by the time it does land, you're just flat out tired. No curiosity, no suspense, no reward.

But everyone tells a run-on story once in a while. Everyone can improve. Don't despair! Telling a story is an evolving process. It's part of our natural experimentation with stories; this is why it's important to have a story buddy on which to test things. As Nietzsche said:

"Ten times a day must you overcome yourself: this promotes a most wholesome weariness and is opium to the soul."

Overcome yourself. As you find, shape, and share your most essential stories, don't let your ego get in the way. Just get back to the task at hand, whether you're inspiring a team, influencing a customer, or raising a round of funding: make your story an even better vehicle for connection and inspiration.

Here are a few ways things can go awry, and some explorations that can set you straight:

1. It's an explanation, not a story.

An explanation doesn't convey a yearning. It doesn't say *why this matters to you*—or to me. There's no suspense, no tension, no gift at the end.

Remember, a story is about somebody who wants something and can't have it. As he struggles to get what he wants, we begin to feel connected to the story.

An explanation doesn't give us a sense of connection. It helps us gather information and organize it in an intelligent and linear way, from beginning to end. But it doesn't cause us to open up or seek the answers ourselves, or feel compelled to go along on a journey. There's no payoff.

So you create a journey. You don't deliver the message at the beginning; instead you let the audience discover the message. If it's an insight that you had, take us to that moment. Were you naive, full of yourself, struggling? Did it send you on a journey? Are you still on that journey? Anchor in time and space, going from one place to another place. Take us there, sparking your listeners' curiosity, so they lean forward and ask:

And then what happened?

And then offer what you have learned. What has changed?

The next day, even though they've forgotten the thousands of bits of information and the handful of explanations they received the day before, as they sit down for a cup of coffee, they will still feel the power of that story.

2. You skipped past the trial.

Maybe your story seems too heavy or too long, and you don't want to bring your audience into the details of your trial. So maybe you skip the really hard part and get right to the change. Resist the temptation. Rarely is it simply about achieving a goal. A story takes us through an experience of discovery. So own the trial! Show us how you (or the character) paid for the experience with her or his blood, sweat, tears, sleep, stress, sorrow, and challenge.

Don't just tell us how the world is different now. If the story feels a bit fast, or too zoomed out, consider how you might better illuminate the trial. Show us how things were before. Go back to the beginning—before the problem started—and reconsider. Something happened to send you on this journey. What was that something? What did you (or the main character) believe? Was there an *and then one day* that dropped you into a challenge? Did you have an *until finally* moment, where things really had to change?

Our trials often become our best allies in achieving our goals later in life, and they also make for the best stories. Because, after all . . . you must have survived, otherwise you wouldn't be telling the story.

3. You're stuck in the middle of the story.

Your character faced the problem, and the problem was real, and it was difficult, very difficult in fact, and . . . well that's it. If your story is burdened with a struggle that isn't resolved, you miss an opportunity. And the story, whether from an experience that happened recently or one that happened a long time ago, may not quite be ready to tell. This may be. Do you ever hear a tale like this:

I was feeling really out of shape. So I started walking a little more, and cutting out my afternoon muffin. After two weeks, nothing changed. Then, I stopped walking. And it's been a month now, and nothing has changed.

Waiting . . . waiting . . . um . . . *why are you telling me this?* We all, of course, can benefit from an opportunity to share our challenging experiences. But it's not simply the facing the challenge that makes a good story. It's the process of discovery that comes with it. The tension releases cortisol, so we pay attention. The suspense releases dopamine, and then with the conclusion the cortisol is eased, and we feel the oxytocin. *Ahh.*

We appreciate that payoff.

If your goal is to connect with your audience and to convey meaning, then there should be some other side of the journey— even if it is simply a stated commitment.

If the lesson of your story is in your recovery from a ski injury, and you don't want to tell about how you were checking your phone and slammed your shoulder into a tree, and instead you just say "I was skiing and I got hurt," we may not be not able to hear the rest of your story because our minds are stuck on questions. *Wait, what happened? What does she mean by hurt? How did she get hurt? Why does this matter?* And your point is going to be lost in the shuffle. I'm not saying over-share. But sometimes personal stories require some vulnerability to reveal true change.

4. You missed the lesson.

Recently, I was training a group of leaders at a San Francisco-based insurance company. Mitra, one of the most revered sales leaders in the company, raised her hand to talk about a deal that had fallen apart in a boardroom. She had some reluctance to tell her story, and yet this was overcome by her desire not to repeat the experience. She had great curiosity about how to view the story, to understand how to tell it, and, most importantly, how to learn the lesson herself. We workshopped the challenge as a group and then moved on to the next exercise.

But to my surprise, people didn't want to move on to another exercise. They kept coming back to Mitra's story, with questions, ideas, and suggestions. This was in part due to her consistent sales success—the others were curious about the challenges she had faced—and in part due to her willingness to be vulnerable about the topic. But it's also because one story connects to another—the personal becomes universal.

Mitra's story was both powerful and emblematic. Everyone in the room saw himself or herself in this one challenge, and the experience became both a go-to for Mitra and a valued impact story for the group. Mitra was also hooked on how powerful it is to transform your stories—and she's now working adamantly to develop her repertoire.

So ask yourself as you scan your stories: *Did I learn anything? Am I working to change something every day?* Your story doesn't have to have a clear end. It doesn't have to be the same loss and lesson as everyone else—it just has to connect to *why things are different now.* It has to offer some perspective.

If we only know what you do, and don't know *why* you do it, or we know your title but not *how you got here*, we might be sympathetic, but we're not going to be motivated. So drop us into the challenge, and bring us back up with the lesson.

Add to your repertoire. Develop your stories. And as you gather them in your quiver and hone them, practice different ways of telling them to match the need of the occasion.

A story is not about data.
It is about connection
made real. It is about
meaning. Your story
provides a way of
knowing, one that tells
us why things are as
they are. It is your calling
card in a world that is
always listening.

Afterword

THE JOURNEY AHEAD

Storytelling is a *practice*. It's not a *perfect*. Like yoga or golf or speaking Italian or planting fruit trees, it takes time and attention. And dedication pays dividends, because your stories are always changing as you discover new insights, new lessons, new audiences with different needs, and new applications.

It's been a long time now since I began this project. A long time since I rode up into the Berkeley hills and was swept into the story of an ancient king who was lost at sea. Many studies, many struggles, and many scribbles have since been left in my wake. And while it's been a long journey, I feel as if I have only just begun.

Each step I've taken along the path to bringing you this book—including some that gave me insight into how a story works, what we remember, how to capture and hold our essential lessons, and how to shape them—revealed new trails, new twists and turns, and new stories. And yet I feel as if I have only scratched the surface. So this is my humble offering, and I hope it has had a positive impact on you.

Perhaps, as a result of your excursion into the territories of *Retellable*, you've found that by anchoring in the sensory details of a key moment, you can draw your audience into the story. Or that just a bit of suspense can transform a seemingly simple realization into a valuable story. Perhaps, from now on, you'll think about the Journey Curve when you hear stories, asking the question: *Where was the change?* Perhaps your ears will perk up when you hear the words *and then one day.*

Perhaps a tip from this book will help you land your keynote in such a way that the audience feels truly inspired, or help you address your team during a critical juncture at an all-hands meeting. Perhaps one story will help you hold your wisdom in a new and lasting way, and others will be inspired by your stories. Perhaps you'll be showered with praise, or with props, or with profits.

Playing the realist, though, you may only have the energy to plant some seeds right now and just a bit of time to tend them. Maybe you tell one story or two and forget about developing your other stories for a while. The good news, however, is that stories aren't suddenly going to go away. As long as you care, and you listen, nature will do her work: the rains will come, and the sun, and one day in the future you'll be happily surprised to see your stories have grown new branches and bore new fruits. You'll tell them, and in turn they'll be retold.

In time, my hope is that you will learn to more clearly recognize the values of a good story, and to hold it in your hands. That you'll care for your stories, and that they will transform your life and the lives of those around you. Because what better thing, really, do we have to offer our audiences than the deepest wisdom we have discovered in our journeys, applied at a moment when it is most needed?

As a result you will become a better storyteller, and a better leader. And my hope is that bit-by-bit, your stories—and the actions that give them further life—will help create the world you're wishing to see.

And so, dear reader, if you have only three minutes, right now, to tell your most important story to your audience, whether it be a crowd in a conference hall or the person standing in front of you holding a cocktail, what will you tell? Will you detail your accomplishments? Will you list off data that proves the point you want to convey? Or will you offer them a little magic, a small seed that might just be alive tomorrow?

Time, it seems, will retell.

ACKNOWLEDGMENTS

Without a chance meeting with storyteller Joel ben Izzy in Saul's Deli one winter's afternoon in Berkeley, California, I'm certain this book would never have been written. Joel's wisdom and endless enthusiasm on the workings of story have had a life-changing impact on me, and have clearly served as the catalyst for this book. So I offer a great bow toward the hills of Berkeley, where he is undoubtedly contemplating one of the thousands of stories that live in his mind and memory.

Without the patience and perseverance of my wife, Ahrona, who helped me keep the ship afloat through the ups and downs of navigating a new niche in an ancient territory, this book would have never have been written. So thank you, Ahrona Joy, my travel partner, for your resilience, faith, and ability to dream. Thanks, too, for supporting my habit of swimming in the chilly waters of the Bay when I most needed to hit the restart button.

Without the patience and support of my parents, Burt and Maxine, who have always helped me believe in a world that hasn't yet been born, and who have endured all my travels and travails with cheers from the sidelines, this book would never have been written.

But it was. It's a done *something*, words and ideas and teachings folded into a package. So I want to state my appreciation for anyone who has set out to write a book. I used to look at a book that didn't seem interesting and say, well, that book kind of stunk. And now I look at those books and say, holy cow, these people rose before the sun—or stayed awake long after it was down—and mapped out their ideas and refined them over and over, and rewrote and rewrote and rewrote and got feedback again and again and got hammered in edits and, well, you get the point. These authors cared enough to bring their ideas to life.

Thanks to Yiying Lu for conjuring up such a potent logo, and to Sasha Wizansky for your dedicated and clean design work. Thanks to Nora for your guidance and patience on the long and winding edit, and thanks to Jed Miller, Pete-O McLaughlin, Arpad Molnar, Rich Singer, Lisa Poulson, Jason Pair, and Jill Wesley for your timely support and critical refinements that were so instrumental in the process. Gratitude to Jonah Sachs for your wise insights and prodding on the Journey Curve—they impact me every day. Thanks to Michael Margolis and David Nihill for sharing your lessons from your own adventures into this wild world of book creation. Thanks to Ken and Maddy for your eternal enthusiasm for what's possible.

Humble thanks to my mentors on the long journey: Miakoda Taylor, Larry Ware, Ellen McGirt, and of course my brother Dane Golden. Thanks to my men's group, who prodded me onward when I was stuck on some unknown island, looking under rocks and roots for clues on how to proceed. That's you, David Doostan, Zelig Golden, Ben Ringler, Doug Chermak, David Miller and Simcha Schwartz. Endless gratitude to my in-laws, Marc, Jackie and Nate, who have gone above and beyond the call of family at every turn.

Thank you Joseph Campbell and Kurt Vonnegut, oh how I'd love to sit down over a Scotch with you both just about now.

Finally, to those teachers too numerous to name, whose wisdom and challenges and stories have propelled me here: I thank you.

Berkeley, Fall 2016

NOTES

1. Nick Bilton, "The American Diet: 34 Gigabytes a Day," *New York Times*, December 9, 2009, accessed May 10, 2016, http://bits.blogs.nytimes.com/2009/12/09/the-american-diet-34-gigabytes-a-day/.

2. Véronique Boulenger et al., "Grasping Ideas with the Motor System: Semantic Somatotopy in Idiom Comprehension," *Cerebral Cortex* 19, no. 8 (2009): 1905–14.

3. Chip Heath and Dan Heath, *Made to Stick: Why Some Ideas Survive and Others Die* (New York: Random House, 2007), 242–43.

4. Uri Hasson et al., "Speaker-Listener Neural Coupling Underlies Successful Communication," *Proceedings of the National Academy of Sciences* 107, no. 32 (2010): 14425–30.

5. Matthias Gruber et al., "States of Curiosity Modulate Hippocampus-Dependent Learning via the Dopaminergic Circuit," Neuron 84, no. 2 (2014), 486–96.

6. Paul J. Zak et al., "Oxytocin Increases Generosity in Humans," *PLOS ONE* 2, no. 11 (2007): e1128, accessed May 1,

2016, doi:10.1371/journal.pone.0001128.

7. "Andrew Stanton: The Clues to a Great Story," accessed
    May 22, 2016, https://www.ted.com/talks/andrew_stanton_
    the_clues_to_a_great_story.

8. Lisa Cron, *Wired for Story: The Writer's Guide to Using Brain
    Science to Hook Readers from the Very First Sentence* (Berke-
    ley: Ten Speed Press, 2012), 9.

9. "Elon Musk Debuts the Tesla Powerwall," accessed May 1,
    2016, https://www.youtube.com/watch?v=yKORsrlN-2k.

10. James E. Short, "How Much Media?" study, Institute for Com-
    munications Technology Management, Marshall School of
    Business, University of Southern California (2103), 7.

11. "Kurt Vonnegut on the Shapes of Stories," accessed June 1,
    2016, https://www.youtube.com/watch?v=oP3c1h8v2ZQ.

12. "22 #storybasics I've picked up in my time at Pixar," ac-
    cessed May 2, 2016, http://storyshots.tumblr.com/post/
    25032057278/22-storybasics-ive-picked-up-in-my-time-
    at-pixar.

13. Christopher Vogler, *The Writer's Journey: Mythic Struc-
    ture for Writers* (Studio City, CA: M. Wiese Productions,
    1998), 143.

14. "Model 200B audio oscillator, 1939," accessed May 15, 2016.
    http://www.hp.com/hpinfo/abouthp/histnfacts/museum/
    earlyinstruments/0008/index.html.

15. "The Last Refuge," accessed July 1, 2016, http://www.pbs.org/
    nationalparks/history/ep2/.

16. "A Dozen Things I've Learned from Ben Horowitz about
    Management, Investing, and Business," accessed July 1, 2016,
    https://25iq.com/2015/07/05/a-dozen-things-ive-learned-
    from-ben-horowitz-about-management-investing-and-
    business/.

17. Jonah Sachs, *Winning the Story Wars: Why Those Who*

Tell—and Live—the Best Stories Will Win The Future (Boston: Harvard Business School Publishing, 2012), 153.

18. "Martin Luther King Jr.: I Have a Dream," accessed June 1, 2016, http://www.americanrhetoric.com/speeches/mlkihaveadream.htm.

19. "1983 Apple Keynote—The '1984' Ad Introduction," accessed May 1, 2016, https://www.youtube.com/watch?v=lSiQA6KKyJo.

20. James Joyce, *The Trieste Notebook*, page 96, 1907.

21. "Becky Tarbotton—Rainforest Action Network—REVEL 2012," accessed May 16, 2016, https://www.youtube.com/watch?v=eAcAlxn-mCk.

22. Joshua Foer, *Moonwalking with Einstein: The Art and Science of Remembering* (New York: Penguin Books, 2011), 90.

23. "How Stories Change the Brain," accessed July 1, 2016. http://greatergood.berkeley.edu/article/item/how_stories_change_brain.

24. "Our Story," accessed September 1, 2016. https://www.enterprisecommunity.org/sites/default/files/media-library/about/enterprise-our-story.pdf.

ADDITIONAL RESOURCES

Campbell, Joseph. *The Hero with a Thousand Faces*. Princeton, NJ: Princeton Press. 1968.

ben Izzy, Joel. *The Beggar King and the Secret of Happiness*. Chapel Hill, NC: Algonquin Books, 2005.

King, Stephen. *On Writing: A Memoir of the Craft*. New York: Simon and Schuster, 2000.

Nihill, David. *Do You Talk Funny? 7 Comedy Habits to Become a Better (and Funnier) Public Speaker*. Dallas: BenBella Books, 2016.

Sachs, Jonah. *Winning the Story Wars: Why Those Who Tell—and Live—the Best Stories Will Win The Future*. Boston: Harvard Business School Publishing, 2012.

Shaw, Tahir. *In Arabian Nights: A Caravan of Moroccan Dreams*. New York: Bantam Books, 2007.

Erickson, Gary. *Raising the Bar: Integrity and Passion in Life and Business: The Story of Clif Bar Inc.* San Francisco: Jossey-Bass, 2004

The hero is the one who comes to know.

—Joseph Campbell

AUTHOR'S BIO

Jay Golden is an author, storyteller, and founder of Retellable (formerly Wakingstar Storyworks), a boutique story consulting and training company based in the San Francisco Bay Area. For 10 years, Jay has coached leaders, led trainings, and crafted stories for clients such as Facebook, LinkedIn, YouTube, and Rainforest Action Network. His new book, also entitled *Retellable*, explores how stories work and how leaders can use them to deliver key insights and catalyze change.

Jay has spoken on CNN, Fox News, and at the Conference on World Affairs. When he's not working, Jay can be found walking the hills, swimming the bay, or sharing stories with his wife and two kids.

[Free] Radical
Anything that doesn't kill you

Made Strong